THE LESSON PLANNING
HANDBOOK

Essential Strategies That Inspire Student Thinking & Learning

PETER BRUNN

Foreword by Carl Anderson

SCHOLASTIC

New York • Toronto • London • Auckland • Sydney
Mexico City • New Delhi • Hong Kong • Buenos Aires

DEDICATION

For Nina—ily

Editor: Lois Bridges

Production management: Amy Rowe

Cover design: Brian LaRossa

Interior design: Sydney Wright

Copy editor: Eileen Judge

ISBN-13: 978-0-545-08745-2
ISBN-10: 0-545-08745-7

Copyright © 2010 by Peter Brunn

Contents

Acknowledgments

The seed for this book was planted in New York City. It was there that Lucy Calkins graciously invited me to join Columbia University's Teachers College Reading and Writing Project. Lucy opened my eyes to what is possible in classrooms and I still carry her voice with me today. It was during my time at the Project that I met Carl Anderson. Carl's work continues to inspire me, and I am honored that he wrote the foreword to this book.

I could never have completed this project without the support of my colleagues at the Developmental Studies Center. Eric Schaps and Frank Snyder both gave me the freedom and support to write this book. Shaila Regan and Susie Alldredge taught me most of what I know about staff development. My colleagues Thuy Do and Christine Venturis were the first "outside" readers of this manuscript. I treasure their ideas and their friendship. Sue Wilder and Jan Berman gave valuable feedback on early drafts. Grady Carson, Kelly Stuart, Martha Twitchell, Linda Rourke, Ginger Cook, Susan Young, Isabel Mclean, and Martha Morgan all contributed enormously to my thinking. Ben Brady and all of DSC's independent representatives have been incredibly supportive.

This book began when Laura Robb kindly told her editor at Scholastic that I might be someone worth talking with. For this, I will forever be grateful. At Scholastic, I want to thank Virginia Dooley for green-lighting this project, Gloria Pipkin for thoughtful manuscript feedback, Amy Rowe for shepherding the book through production, Brian LaRossa for crafting the stunning pink cover, and Sydney Wright for designing these gorgeous pages. Most importantly, I am indebted to my editor, Lois Bridges, for believing in me and being so patient, wise, and kind.

I wish to thank my parents, Don and Judy, for nurturing in me the confidence to write this book. I also want to thank my mother-in-law and father-in-law, Nobuko and John, and my sister and brother-in-law, Anna and Marc, for taking care of my family whenever work took me away from home.

Finally, I want to thank my daughter, Karina, and my wife, Nina, for enduring my long absences while I worked in schools or sequestered myself away to write. I promise Karina that now we can ride our bikes again and take no-way-walks together. And I thank Nina, who is my best friend and partner. She nudged me when I needed to move and listened when I was stuck. Her teaching continues to inspire me and is embedded in every corner of this book. This book is as much hers as it is mine. I thank them both for making me who I am.

The Lesson Planning Handbook: Essential Strategies That Inspire Student Thinking & Learning

Foreword

When I was a new teacher, I planned my lessons for the upcoming week on Sunday evenings. In my plan book, I wrote down what content I hoped to cover each day of the week for each subject that I taught. I loved the way the pages of my plan book looked when they were neatly filled out. I was filled with a sense that I was a good teacher because my plans were so thorough.

I still had a lot to learn. Back then, I thought it was enough to plan the content of my teaching. I quickly learned that this wasn't enough, as evidenced by my students' reactions to my lessons, which was often indifference, sometimes even confusion. I didn't yet know that to be a good teacher, there were other dimensions of teaching I needed to incorporate into my lesson planning that would help to engage students, and give them the opportunity to learn.

In the wise, clear, and practical *Lesson Planning Handbook*, Peter Brunn teaches us what it truly means to plan for effective teaching. In a time when we as a profession have a wealth of books that suggest lesson after lesson to teach, how important it is we have this book to focus us on *how* to teach these lessons in ways that truly help students become strong readers and writers.

So many aspects of *The Lesson Planning Handbook* will be valuable to new and experienced teachers alike. The central idea of the book is about changing our teaching stance. By this, Brunn means that not only do we need to plan the content of our teaching, we also need to plan with the students we're teaching in mind. As Brunn explains, how we take into account what we know and learn about students before and as we teach a lesson are critical to the ultimate success of our teaching.

Teachers will also find Brunn's discussion of how to structure lessons helpful. In this section, Brunn makes transparent one of the key skills of highly effective teaching, and makes this skill accessible to everyone. The insights that he shares about structuring lessons can help us transform our teaching from pedestrian to magical.

Brunn fills the book with the lessons he's learned as an elementary school teacher and as a staff developer at the Teachers College Reading and Writing Project and the Developmental Studies Center. These experiences give the book the ring of authenticity. Reading the book, you'll have no doubt Peter has been in the classroom, and continues to be there day after day.

If only *The Lesson Planning Handbook* had been published two decades ago when I started teaching! But it's here for us now, and from reading and applying what we learn, our lessons will be stronger, and, most important, our students will be engaged learners in our classrooms.   —Carl Anderson, 2009

Introduction

"I want all our children to go to schools worthy of their potential—schools that challenge them, inspire them, and instill in them a sense of wonder about the world around them."

—President Barack Obama, in an open letter
to his daughters in *Parade* magazine,
January 18, 2009

Sunday mornings are special in my house. We call them "Pancake Sundays." Our extended family often comes over, and we all share breakfast before we go our separate ways and begin the day. But before everyone arrives and the chaos of a big family breakfast starts, we enjoy quiet time. I get to read the paper, maybe do some writing, or, better yet, just sit on the couch with my daughter, Karina, and watch old *Tom and*

Jerry cartoons. Sometimes I balance my computer on my lap and try to do all three. On the Sunday just before the presidential inauguration, as I browsed the paper, I stumbled across the quotation above from President Obama. As soon as I read it, I grabbed my computer and recorded it. Maybe I was just swept away in the emotion of that historic week, but as I read that open letter from our new president to his daughters, I got choked up. I was filled with hope for our schools and for our profession. This, I thought, is why I became a teacher in the first place.

Reflecting on President Obama's words brings me back to my first few years of teaching. When I started my career as a teacher in the South Bronx, my teaching was a long ways from "inspirational." I spent more time trying to get students to sit down and get along with one another than I did trying to "instill in them a sense of wonder about the world around them." I loved my students, I wanted to be a thoughtful teacher, but I was frustrated. At the same time, I knew that if I did not improve my teaching, I would end up being callous to my students and disliking my job. It was about this time that a colleague sat me down and said, "Just listen to them, Peter. Really listen to them. Deep down they want to do their best. If you really listen, they will tell you what they need." At the time I heard this I smiled, but had no earthly idea what he meant.

But I managed to keep teaching. Over time, I began to see clues as to what he was trying to tell me. I needed to trust my students. I needed to trust that they were doing their best, that they all could do the work, and that they wanted to learn. I needed to listen to them—"really listen." I also began to recognize that it was not me, the teacher, and them, the students. There was only us. If real learning was going to take place, we had to do it together. I began to see teaching as a dynamic relationship. I eventually realized that maintaining this relationship, like all relationships, meant that I had to be a better listener. It changed the way I planned and taught my lessons. All of this created a seismic shift in my teaching stance.

That we need to change our stance as teachers is the primary message of this book. To that end, my goal is to share how to listen closely in order to access and understand students' thinking. I will demonstrate how to construct lessons where we can focus on how our students are making sense of rigorous content. I present techniques for visualizing how our lessons might unfold and for anticipating the challenges we will inevitably face. Finally, and most important, this book is about inspiring students to investigate the wondrous world around them.

> That we need to change our stance as teachers is the primary message of this book. To that end, my goal is to share how to listen closely in order to access and understand students' thinking.

GOALS OF THE BOOK

At the Developmental Studies Center I am lucky to work with a team of staff developers who regularly meet to refine our work with schools. Much of the content for this book comes directly from these conversations about the strategies that have had the biggest effect on the classrooms in which we work. While I don't want to oversimplify the complex job we have as teachers, I have tried to keep the focus of this book on two fundamental issues: planning and facilitating our lessons. Focusing on these two areas has paid the biggest dividends in our work. It has been a transforming experience for many teachers. Therefore, this book aims to do the following:

- Share common qualities of successful reading and writing lessons
- Offer a structure for organizing lessons across the school day that optimizes student thinking
- Outline a process for planning, reviewing, and revising lessons that fosters student thinking and interaction

* Provide techniques for facilitating rich and meaningful lessons with students

Using the Book

This book can be read in a variety of ways. Teachers who are new to the profession might want to read the book in the order in which it is written. Going through the material in this way provides the most support for teachers new to planning lessons. It might also be helpful to read the book with a trusted colleague. This will allow you both to try out the lesson planning and facilitation techniques described here and then discuss together how it went.

More experienced teachers and study groups will want to read the book in parts. Whether you are using a workshop approach in your classroom or a more traditional basal program, the chapters are designed to help you deepen your interaction with students.

Summary

There is no magic formula for crafting lessons that shine. Good teaching is not a mystical art, nor does it happen by chance. Powerful instruction occurs only through the hard work of an experienced and thoughtful teacher. The chapters in this book are designed to make explicit some of the implicit teaching moves that lead to lessons full of student thinking. It is a book I wish I had had during my first years as a struggling teacher in the Bronx. It is my hope that this book serves as a tool to help you take the small steps toward your vision of what is possible for you and your students.

PART I

Teaching Essentials

This section outlines ten key actions for teachers to consider before, during, and after teaching lessons.

Chapter 1

Ten Qualities of Successful Lessons

Not long ago I was working to support reading coaches in Missouri. On one visit, I observed reading comprehension lessons in two third-grade classrooms. While both teachers taught the same lesson from their reading program, the outcomes were markedly different. One lesson was wonderfully successful, rich with student thinking and interaction. Students were engaged, they worked together, and they were involved in lively discussion and debate. The other lesson was dull and unsuccessful. The students said and did very little while the teacher talked a great deal and did lots of work. There was little evidence of student achievement or growth. When I reflected on this visit with the school's reading coaches in the library after school, we agreed that the first teacher possessed unique skills and strategies that allowed her to make successful teaching moves in her lesson—qualities that were absent in the other teacher's lesson. This raised an essential question for our work. If the content of their lessons was the same, what exactly were they doing that made such a difference in the students' thinking? How could we identify for teachers the powerful moves that greatly affect the outcome of our teaching?

While there is no easy answer to this question, it is clear that successful lessons showcase teacher actions that set them apart from unsuccessful ones. As we learned from our work, these actions cannot be scripted in a program. It is the way in which the lesson is planned, structured, and facilitated that makes the difference. To find these qualities, we need to look between the lines of programs and written lesson plans.

Successful lessons result when teachers do the following:

- Plan lessons with their *students* in mind (not just the content)
- Use a predictable lesson structure that allows students to grow academically *and* socially
- Make listening to students' thinking the heart of their lessons
- Keep the body of their lessons focused on open-ended topics
- Never lose track of the lesson's objective
- Use facilitation techniques to probe student thinking

Students also play active roles in successful lesson implementation. Effective lessons engage students by giving them opportunities to do the following:

- Do most of the talking
- Work independently
- Develop social skills for successful peer interaction
- Experience a sense of community

Over the past three years, my colleagues Christine Venturis and Thuy Do and I have mined our notes to identify these successful teacher actions. We also met with trusted teachers, literacy coaches, and district administrators to identify key actions from their work. Including them in the work we do with schools has made a tremendous difference in the success of the educators with whom we consult. These actions also set the stage for the rest of the chapters in this book   .

Action #1   Teachers plan lessons with their *students* in mind (not just the content).

When I started out teaching, my friend and colleague Stephen used to sit with me and listen patiently to what I planned to teach. I was teaching first grade, and he was working with sixth and seventh graders. I was taking graduate classes at Teachers College at the time, and he was always interested in what I was trying out. During these talks, I would pull out my plans and share what I intended to teach. I would say, "We're working on memoirs, so tomorrow I'm going to teach the 'show not tell' writing strategy from Ralph Fletcher's book *What a Writer Needs*." Or I would say, "I am going to use Mem Fox's book *Tough Boris* to show how we make inferences in our reading."

These were great teaching ideas. In looking back, however, what stands out is that in all the cases, I talked mostly about the content I planned to cover. Rarely did I discuss *whom* I was teaching.

Our plans are incomplete if we do not consider both the students and the content. Despite being under a great deal of pressure to cover content, and despite facing test scores published in local newspapers, we must resist the

> Despite being under a great deal of pressure to cover content, and despite facing test scores published in local newspapers, we must resist the temptation to plow through content if we want to conduct powerful lessons.

temptation to plow through content if we want to conduct powerful lessons. After all, what good is touching upon every detail of a unit of study if, in the end, students don't understand it?

Whom we are teaching must be an explicit part of our lesson plans. Now when I am getting ready for a lesson, for instance, I must think about challenges my English language learners might face. I ask myself, Do they need more background knowledge than other students in the room? Are there idioms in this text that might trip them up? I also reflect on struggling students. Do they need to do this activity in a smaller group? Is this text too difficult to serve as a model for the whole class? In short, I am really asking myself, What do I know about my student as learners? and How might this knowledge affect my lesson plan? When we plan lessons with students in mind, we take actions such as these:

- Pause in places where we know they might struggle

- Spend more time building concepts they don't know—even if this means not getting through all of the day's content

- Move quickly through content students already know

Action #2 | Teachers use a predictable lesson structure that allows students to grow academically *and* socially.

When I walk into Lisa Billings's third-grade classroom in Louisville, Kentucky, I am always amazed by how smooth her teaching is. There is a beautiful rhythm to it. I love the way she gathers the students and uses signals to get their attention. I also appreciate how she makes sure each lesson includes time to set up and prepare students for how they will work together. There is always time for students to work in small groups and to work independently. She closes every lesson with a reflection on how students worked together. By doing this at a predictable time each day, her students seem to know what is coming next, and they are completely prepared for it. Her lessons hum with student activity. The structure of her teaching helps her students know what to expect and keeps her teaching clear and organized.

When lessons have a rhythm and a structure and appropriate procedures are in place, distractions are minimized and students can better focus on the tasks at hand. With disruptions kept to a minimum, we can better listen to students and focus our teaching on their thinking.

Predictable structures accomplish the following:

- Provide the glue that holds our lessons together
- Give the teacher a consistent path for introducing the academic and social content
- Provide time for independent and small-group work
- Create the space for students to reflect after the lesson on their academic work and social interactions
- Minimize distractions and interruptions
- Keep lessons focused on student thinking

ᴀᴄᴛɪᴏɴ #3   Teachers make listening to students' thinking the heart of their lessons.

Student thinking lies at the heart of our teaching. Their thinking—our essential resource—powers all the work in our classroom, but it easily disappears if we are not keen enough to pay attention. Susie Alldredge, primary author of the reading comprehension program Making Meaning, once said to me, as I was planning a workshop, "You know, if we could just help teachers listen closely to their students' thinking, it would make a big difference. It would change how they teach." Susie recognizes that all too often, in our rush to get through our material, we don't spend enough time on our students' sense-making.

The advent of high-stakes testing coupled with mandated district benchmark assessments have pressured many teachers to narrow their teaching to cover only tested facts (Alvarez & Corn, 2008). In many of our classrooms, this has had disastrous effects on teaching and learning. Learning becomes about memorizing content and not about developing ideas—certainly not about student thinking. Monitoring student thinking can help us resist reducing our teaching in this way.

Monitoring student thinking is not as simple as opening our eyes and ears. It may start there, but it also involves being very intentional about how and where we get the data that tells us what is happening in our students' minds. This means that in most lessons I try to construct opportunities for students to make their thinking public. I then make sure to collect these public artifacts so I can craft a mosaic of the thinking they are doing in my room. Here are some examples of these artifacts.

- **Notes from conferences or whole-group conversations.** When we pull up next to a young reader or writer and ask questions about his or her work, we get a great deal of data about what is happening for the student. If we listen closely in these conferences, we will learn what students remember from the lessons we have taught, where they are struggling, and what they can do well.

- **Students' entries in a writer's notebook.** Writer's notebooks are filled with evidence of student thinking. Each entry comes after one of our thoughtful lessons and allows us to peek into how students are making sense of what the class is working on.

- **Marks students make on their drafts of writing.** When students begin to revise their writing, we often have them mark their drafts in places where they plan to make their piece better. They may place a sticky note on a section where they want to add more details. They may write another ending in the margin, or they may circle words they want to make more interesting. These markings are critical for us to understand the decisions they are making in their writing.

- **Sticky notes that students place in their independent reading books.** Notes that students post in their independent reading books are full of information about what they are thinking as they read stories and nonfiction texts. They are indispensable to me in getting a picture of how students are making sense of the lessons that I have taught.

- **Reader response journals.** The writing that students do after they read can be tailored to showcase how they are making sense of their texts.

- **Teacher's notes from students' conversations** in whole-group, small-group, or partner conversations.

There are many other forms of data and ways to collect it. In their book *Kidwatching*, Gretchen Owocki and Yetta Goodman note that "sometimes you capture observations through anecdotal notes, while other times you collect artifacts such as oral reading samples, taped recordings of children's reading, retellings, responses to literature, writing samples, answers to interview questions, and children's self reflections on their learning" (p. 8). Regardless of the data you collect, what is important is that you have an organized plan for obtaining and analyzing it.

Action #4 Teachers keep the body of their lessons focused on open-ended topics.

Our best teaching occurs when students spend most of the lesson time engaged in meaningful thinking and interaction. Instead of marching students to one right answer, or having them memorize and regurgitate lists of facts, our most successful lessons have students mucking around in places where there might be disagreement, tension, and multiple interpretations of concepts and ideas. I can remember when my students and I examined Ken Mochizuki's book *Baseball Saved Us*. This is a powerful story about a Japanese American boy who was forced with his family into an internment camp during World War II. After I read the story to my class and we discussed it a bit, I held up the book and showed the title. I said, "Let's look again at the title. Some of you thought it was an interesting name for the book." I then read the title—*Baseball Saved Us.* I asked, "So, who was saved?" The students then spent lots of time thinking about who, in fact, was saved by baseball in the story. Was it the boy? Was it Japanese Americans? Or was it our society as a whole? Because there was no clear "right" answer, students had to use evidence from the text to justify their opinions to one another.

> Our best teaching occurs when students spend most of the lesson time engaged in meaningful thinking and interaction.

I could have simply asked who the main characters were and asked them how they liked the book. But by focusing the discussion on an open-ended question—"So, who was saved?"—we were able to get much deeper into the text and more fully explore the issues presented. These open-ended lessons are powerful because they involve these qualities.

- **Rigorous thinking.** In open-ended lessons, students' ideas encounter lots of scrutiny from their peers.
- **Creativity.** Allowing for multiple interpretations encourages students to think outside the box.
- **Risk taking.** Open-ended lessons encourage students to share untested ideas with their peers, even those who may be at different academic levels from themselves.

We know lessons are working when . . .

- Students do most of the talking
- Students listen to the teacher and to one another respectfully
- Students' talk and work is on task
- The teacher asks mostly open-ended questions
- The teacher paces the lesson

Action #5 Teachers never lose track of the lesson's objective.

It is easy to get lost in our lessons. We often lose focus of our teaching objectives, even during our lesson-planning process. I recently met with a group of fifth-grade teachers who were planning a comprehension lesson using *Star of Fear, Star of Hope*, a picture book by Jo Hoestlandt, set in France during World War II. One of the planning issues the teachers faced was how much preteaching to do about the war and the Holocaust. They knew their students did not have much background knowledge on the war. Some teachers argued that they should spend time discussing the Holocaust. Others argued that background knowledge was not important in understanding this particular story so they should not spend time on it. Finally, one of the teachers said, "What's our objective here? If this is a comprehension lesson, then we should spend our time getting into the text. If we spend 25 minutes building background knowledge— background that our students might not fully need—then we won't have time to get into the story itself." After some back and forth, the group decided that because the book made it pretty clear what was happening to the Jews in the story, they did not have to spend much time on it beforehand. Instead they found a middle ground. They decided to spend a few minutes giving enough critical details on the war so students could access the text. They would revisit the bigger topics of war and the Holocaust at another time.

I thought this was smart planning. Together the teachers made some difficult decisions. Like the group of colleagues above, we must sometimes resist the urge to teach everything. This can be hard because we are often faced with many "teachable moments" throughout the lesson and throughout the day. But if we keep the lesson's objective in our minds as we plan, we will make more appropriate decisions about what to cover. We can then come back to concepts we feel we need to cover at a more appropriate time. Keeping the lesson objective in mind as we teach allows us to do the following:

* Pace the lesson appropriately

* Ensure we cover necessary content

* Avoid extraneous details that may confuse our students

Action #6 Teachers use facilitation techniques to probe student thinking.

The way in which we facilitate student talk often determines the eventual success of the lesson. When I step in front of students, the way I ask questions, investigate thinking, and connect ideas makes the difference between a lesson where students do most of the thinking and talking and one where I do most of it. Debbie Miller, in her timely book *Teaching With Intention*, pushes us as teachers to be more thoughtful in the ways in which we use language to support student thinking. She explains that we can plan the content of our lessons but we can't script what our students will do with that content. She says, "But we can plan to be present. We can plan to listen carefully, make sense of what the child has to say for ourselves, and respond in thoughtful and purposeful ways that acknowledge, clarify, honor, and support their efforts and move them forward" (p. 55).

On the one hand, we can ask questions that require specific answers. We can fish around the class using call-and-response questioning until we hear the correct answer and then move on to our next question. These questions usually center on specific tangible content. These are questions like, "Who were the main characters?" and "Does anyone know . . .?"

On the other hand, we can ask questions for which there are multiple answers or interpretations. We might ask, "How is Sophie feeling during this part of the story?" Because there are multiple ways our students might answer this more open-ended question, we can then prompt or push them to explain their thinking. We might say, "What in the text makes you think that?" Then we can ask, "Who might have another opinion?" This kind of facilitation allows us to dig deeper into meaty topics. When we see ourselves as facilitators of lessons, it changes our stance in the classroom. When we facilitate, our lessons become about fostering student thinking and interaction. We move from spending lots of time explaining the lesson's content to engaging students around it.

A teacher who facilitates learning does the following:

- Probes student thinking
- Uncovers students' meaning-making processes
- Uses cooperative structures such as Turn to Your Partner or Think, Pair, Share to increase participation
- Asks open-ended questions (questions that can't be answered by one word or a simple *yes* or *no*)
- Listens to and values student thinking

Cooperative Structures

Turn to Your Partner is a cooperative structure that provides students the chance to discuss a concept or brainstorm ideas. It is a forum for all students to share their ideas quickly.

Think, Pair, Share is similar to Turn to Your Partner. The difference is that students are given some time to think about a concept first, before they talk with a partner. (See page 88 for a more complete explanation of both techniques.)

Action #7   Teachers listen and invite students to do most of the talking.

I once asked my wife, Nina, to come into my classroom and record one of my reading lessons. Nina has taught for years, and we often help each other in our teaching. I wanted to examine the amount of talk I did versus how much my students did. When we met afterward, I was shocked by the results. The transcript showed that I dominated the talk in the lesson. We could not tell, from what little the students said, what they were actually thinking. I had covered the lesson's content, but it was clear that I had no idea what my students were thinking about that content.

This proved to be a good exercise for me, so I continued to have her come back, and we talked about what we were noticing. I knew that if I wanted to get students talking, I had to ask better questions. Instead of simply moving on after a student shared, I needed to ask him or her to "tell me more." I found that I had to pause and listen to students' answers if I wanted to put student thinking at the center of our curriculum. Student talk provides a number of benefits:

- Allows a teacher to discover what his or her students know and where they are struggling

- Gives students a chance to express different ideas and interpretations

- Serves as a window into students' thinking processes

- Gives students a chance to connect with one another

- Supports the growth of more ideas

Action #8 Teachers set up students to work independently.

One of the biggest challenges we face at the beginning of the school year is establishing independent work time. I can remember the first time I asked my fourth graders to do some independent reading. I had just moved up to fourth grade from years of teaching first grade. We were on the rug, having just completed a mini-lesson. It was the first or second week of school, and I said, "Okay, let's get our books out and read for a while." Because the students were so much older than my first graders, I assumed that they could quickly get to their seats and start reading. I was wrong—chaos ensued. Students chose books that were too hard or too easy. Some students made bad choices about whom to sit next to. Others wanted to go to the bathroom. I realized that fourth graders need as much preteaching and practice as first graders to get our reading time up and running.

It is, nonetheless, critical that we establish independent work time in our classrooms early in the school year. During this time, students might read in a book at their independent reading level for 30 minutes. Or, they might write by themselves for 30–45 minutes. It takes lots of time, energy, and patience to help students become self-sufficient; however, the benefits are enormous.

During independent work time, students have the opportunity to do the following.

* **Apply and practice the challenging content we cover at their specific academic level.** If we want students to develop as writers, then they need to do lots of writing. If we want them to become thoughtful readers, then they need to spend lots of time with books to grow and expand what they know. There is no substitute for practice.

* **Gain the stamina they will need to take the high-stakes tests.** Standardized tests require students to read and write independently for extended periods of time (Calkins, Montgomery, Falk, & Santman, 1998; Angelillo, 2005). To be ready to do this kind of work, students need to spend lots of time working independently.

* **Develop and grow their own ideas during this necessary quiet time.** I often underestimated how much time it took to let good ideas grow. Kent, a fourth grader I once taught, is a good example. Kent usually struggled with his work. He also had a ton of energy. When he moved to his seat to work independently, he rarely started working right away. He was easily distracted and he often said out loud, "I don't know what to write about" or "I can't find my book." He said this even though he left the carpet with plenty of ideas in his notebook and his book was always in his work basket. I learned to let the class get quiet and give Kent ten

minutes or so to get into his work. Once the class was working and he had some time to look around, flip through his notebook, or look through his basket, he generally started working. I have had lots of "Kents" over the years. I have found that independent work time is critical for allowing them the space they need to get into their work.

Independent work time also creates the following opportunities for teachers.

- **Teachers can pay attention to individual student thinking.** While students are working independently, we get the valuable opportunity to listen to students individually. We discover how they are making sense of the book they are reading. We can see how and why they decided to change their writing. In many ways, the reading and writing conferences give us a front-row seat to the sense-making students are doing—as they do it.

- **Teachers can assess and support individual students.** Our conferences allow us to see how students are using the content we have taught and to support students when they struggle. It is one way to individualize our instruction effectively.

Action #9 — Teachers help students develop the social skills for successful peer interaction.

I often take visitors to Nina's classroom to witness successful peer interaction. On one particular visit, back when she was teaching first grade, some colleagues and I walked into the classroom while the students were on the carpet listening to a read-aloud. During the read-aloud, Nina stopped and asked her class, "What are you wondering right now? Turn to your partner." Her first graders quickly turned to their partners and immediately engaged in quality conversation. When we left, some of my companions' first comments were "I can't believe how those students talked to one another" and "I can't believe how everyone got along and how they were so respectful of one another."

Nina's students were able to interact in this way because she painstakingly taught them the social skills necessary for successful collaboration; for example, she taught them how to look at one another, how to take turns, and how to add on to one another's thinking. Our students don't necessarily walk into our rooms possessing the language and experience needed for a deep book discussion with a partner or for a peer writing conference. We can, however, help them learn these procedures. Teaching students the skills they need to interact with one another allows us to facilitate lessons in much more meaningful ways.

> Teaching students the skills they need to interact with one another allows us to facilitate lessons in much more meaningful ways.

Action #10   Teachers work with students to create a sense of community.

Jasmine came to me in the fourth grade as a struggling reader. At the beginning of the year, she rarely participated in partner book discussions. At the end of independent reading time, I always had partners share what they were reading. Jasmine was reading books three to four grades below her classmates and she was self-conscious and embarrassed. When she met with a partner, she hid her book and found ways to get her partner to do all the talking. If she did talk, it was never about her book. I realized that if she was going to be able to grow as a reader, she had to share her thinking and work with the class. I knew that we needed to develop a community that supported one another—one in which it was safe for students to be themselves. So I worked hard to give students opportunities to build relationships. I also built up my own relationship with Jasmine. After a month or so of hard work, she started to make some progress. By the end of the year, she had made an amazing leap. While I would love to chalk it all up to my expertise as a reading teacher, I really think it was our community that made the difference.

It was during that particular school year I learned that if we want students to grow and develop, then they are going to have to share ideas that are important to them.

In the second edition of *Mosaic of Thought*, Ellin Keene echoes the importance of the classroom community. She writes that, as a necessary condition for success, "Teachers create a climate of respect and civility using rituals, a predictable schedule, and well-defined procedures for meeting routine needs. They trust children to become increasingly independent and to work together to solve problems" (p. 116). It takes a great deal of courage for students to share an untested idea, openly read a book below their classmates' level, or share their learning insecurities with their peers. They risk looking dumb, saying something perceived as silly, and being alone in their thinking. In order to learn, however, these are the very challenges students need to embrace. Risk taking, essential to growth, thrives in a safe and supportive classroom community where students feel known and accepted.

SUMMARY

Watching a new idea bloom in the minds of children is one of the most rewarding aspects of being a teacher. When rooms buzz with excitement as students work in pairs to understand Lois Lowry's book *The Giver*, solve complex number problems, or provide feedback on each other's written compositions, I still get chills. We are at our best when we design our classrooms so that collaboration, imagination, and community are at the center of classroom life.

Part II will help you plan and incorporate these actions into your lessons. Chapter 2 articulates a structure that will help you hold your lessons together, and Chapter 3 provides you with a way to plan lessons with both students and content in mind.

Note to the reader . . .

As you read this book, I encourage you to examine the suggested actions, strategies, and techniques and compare them with what you already do. In our profession, we are often reluctant to remove specific practices from our current teaching repertoire, while, at the same time, we may pile on new instructional challenges. My advice is simple: Let's avoid cramming our teaching full of divergent techniques and, instead, work to find a few key, successful strategies and use them to their fullest potential.

PART II

Before We Teach

Good teachers make instruction look easy. Sometimes it seems magical. To many teachers, powerful teaching can even be a bit mysterious. Powerful teaching is not easy and certainly does not come from magic. Powerful teaching is the result of intentional teacher planning and deep reflection. We will now examine a predictable structure for lessons (Chapter 2) and a five-step lesson-planning process you can use to plan and revise your lessons (Chapter 3).

Chapter 2

Lesson Structure: The Backbone of Our Teaching

When I began my career as a teacher, I was a bit of a mess. Like most new teachers, I had the best of intentions. I worked around the clock in my effort to be successful, but my lessons were inconsistent. I lacked an internal framework for organizing my instruction, so at times my teaching felt cluttered and unfocused. While I made elaborate lesson plans and had grand objectives, there was no structure holding it all together. By lesson structure, I mean the primary steps of a lesson, from the introduction to the conclusion.

The structures we use in our classrooms are much like our closets at home. Without a place to hang our jackets, shelve our shoes, and store our bags and umbrellas, we'd have a mess as soon as we walked into our home. The closets are a physical structure for keeping our house organized and free of clutter. In our teaching, the structures and procedures we use in our lessons serve the same function. The lesson's structure gives us a place to hang all of the important components of our teaching. It helps keep our lessons clean, clear, and organized. It provides us with an internal template we can draw on as we craft our daily teaching.

IMPORTANCE OF LESSON STRUCTURE

I first started thinking deeply about a lesson's structure when my colleagues and I were writing the reading comprehension program Making Meaning. Making Meaning is a K–8 program with the dual goals of providing students with strategies to make sense of texts as well as giving them opportunities to grow socially and ethically. We searched long and hard for a lesson structure that fit these instructional goals. Because of the variety of skills and strategies we needed to cover, as well as our desire to include time for independent, small-group, and partner work, we wanted something flexible and something that could be used consistently. It needed to contain time and space for lesson elements that were critical to us. We talked about making sure our lessons would meet these criteria:

- Be accessible for all levels of students
- Contain designated places for introducing and reflecting on cooperative work
- Be structured so that students did more thinking and talking than the teacher

* Have time for direct teaching when necessary

* Provide students with opportunities to practice and apply our teaching independently

* Construct authentic opportunities for students to collaborate with one another

The thinking we did to craft a lesson's structure has greatly informed my teaching and staff development. It opened my eyes to the importance of structure. It gave me the container I needed to hold my teaching together.

In this chapter, I will share a four-part lesson structure you can use in your own teaching. In combination, the four parts—preparation for work, whole-class teaching time, independent work time, and lesson reflection—form the backbone of our teaching.

> In combination, the four parts—preparation for work, whole-class teaching time, independent work time, and lesson reflection—form the backbone of our teaching.

Try this . . .

Before you read this next section, jot down the structure of your typical reading or writing lesson. As you read, reflect on how the structure presented here might inform the structure you already use. Ask yourself these questions:

• What would my teaching look like if I were to use a similar predictable structure across content areas?

• How is the structure presented here similar to what I already do?

• How is it different?

• What changes will I make in my teaching?

ANATOMY OF A LESSON'S STRUCTURE

Good lessons have essential parts. Just as our arms and legs hold us up and help us move, so too do a lesson's parts ensure our teaching moves forward. This section outlines the key structures that have worked for my colleagues and me as we struggle to improve our teaching and help students grow as thinkers and learners.

Preparation for Work

Preparing students is an often overlooked part of our lessons. In my experience, however, if we don't have a dedicated time when we prepare students for what lies ahead, we may well encounter problems as we move into the lesson. I can remember back when I was modeling a lesson for a colleague. I went into his classroom to teach a comprehension lesson using a section of the book *Journey* by Patricia MacLachlan. The first page of that book contains a powerful vignette that lures the reader into the text. I read the passage aloud, and after I read the last words "And that was when I hit him," I said, "Jot down what you are thinking about the text right now." As the students started writing, I leaned in to observe some of them. Much to my surprise, I noticed that the students were not quickly jotting down thoughts. Instead, they were taking their time to write complete sentences, making sure to spell everything correctly. It dawned on me that I had not set the lesson up right. I had expected them to quickly get their thinking down on the page. I forgot that there is a big difference between jotting down notes and writing something that you think you have to turn in to the teacher. The students knew that the lesson would require writing. They did not know that the writing was for their eyes only, meant to help them organize their thinking for conversation later. They also had never done this before. Had I modeled note-taking before the lesson started, I could have saved myself from having to talk about it in the middle of the lesson and derailing the students' thinking about the book. Such a pitfall is not uncommon. We get into the body of our teaching and then realize that we need to teach additional key skills or concepts that we forgot to do up front. This is why having a structure in mind is essential when I plan lessons. If the first part of every lesson is dedicated to preparing students to work in the lesson, then I won't leave out this important step. Preparation for work features the following elements:

- ☸ Introduction of the day's objective
- ☸ Connections between new content and prior teaching
- ☸ Instruction or review of necessary skills
- ☸ Construction or review of background knowledge, as needed
- ☸ Preparation for working together

A Note About Lessons and Mini-Lessons

Much of what has been written about lesson structure has come out of the literature describing reading and writing workshops. (Calkins, 1994 & 2001; Atwell, 1998; Cleaveland & Ray, 2004; and Angelillo, 2008, are some examples.) These writers have framed the mini-lesson, helping us immeasurably in understanding both its promise and structure. Mini-lessons are short—usually 10 to 15 minutes. During this time, a teacher directly teaches a skill or strategy. There may be some interactive work, and then students go off and apply the skill in their independent reading or writing. In this book, however, I am talking about a concept bigger than a mini-lesson. I want us to think about the entire reading or writing time from the beginning until it is time for another subject. This is important because when I am out working with teachers, I often see them plan only their mini-lesson or direct teaching time. They are not fully conceptualizing the entire reading or writing time. In a workshop classroom, what I call "whole-class teaching" would be the mini-lesson time.

Whole-Class Teaching Time

Most lessons need a time when the whole class is together. Typically, I gather students together on a rug so I can have them in close proximity to me. The length of whole-class teaching varies, depending on what we are covering. At a minimum, it is a place for us to give directions to the group. Usually, though, we are working on a strategy, skill, or procedure. If you are using a basal program, you will want to choose one or two key objectives from the many listed at the front of each lesson. In a reading or writing workshop, you will also use this time to focus on one big concept. In writing workshop, you might teach a key revision strategy. In reading workshop, you may discuss how good readers go back and reread when they realize they are confused. Regardless of the curriculum you use, most lessons need some "whole-class together time" before students break off to apply new skills or strategies on their own.

Whole-class teaching has a very structured look and feel. It is typically divided into three parts:

* Direct-teaching time

* Student try-outs

* Reflection and segue to independent or small-group work

Direct-Teaching Time

In most lessons, there is a time during which we explain certain concepts or demonstrate a technique. This direct-teaching time may take the form of modeling a strategy, explaining a procedure, or naming a skill or technique students are already doing. There are two ways to structure this time. The decision we make about which way to go will depend on the content we have to cover. Sometimes we will need to do some direct instruction up front before students experience something together. Other times we might find it more beneficial if we set up an experience first and then have some explicit instruction after the experience. Let's look at a couple of examples.

When I am working with students to help them pick a topic to publish in writing workshop, I first model how I do it. I take out my own writing notebook and talk through a process for selecting something important to me. Then I have students sit on the carpet and try together what I modeled. This helps students understand what they will do on their own. Other times, however, we might address a strategy in which it works better to have students do the thinking first.

Recently, I was working in a second-grade class in which we explored the comprehension strategy "making mental images." During my whole-group lesson, I decided to read aloud the picture book *Have You Seen Bugs?* by Joanne Oppenheim. I chose this book specifically because of the brilliant images the words give the reader. Because I wanted the text to give students a picture of what was happening in the book, I decided not to show the pictures. As I read, I paused periodically to have students talk about the images they had in their mind. As they talked, I probed their thinking by asking what words in the text helped give them their picture. At the conclusion of the lesson, I talked about how using the words in the story to make a picture of what is happening in your mind is something good readers do. In this version of direct teaching, I ask students to do most of the thinking.

It is important to note that during our direct-teaching time we want to explain only ideas and concepts that students won't be able to get on their own. We don't want to take learning opportunities away from students. If, for instance, we can set up a lesson so that students work with the essential ideas and concepts before we do lots of talking or modeling, we put the responsibility for learning on their shoulders. In both of the lessons described above, I tried to construct lessons that contained enough direct teaching to give students a clear idea of what was expected. But I also wanted to be careful to make sure I did not do the thinking for the students when I did not have to.

In the "making mental images" lesson, I let the words in the book give students the image in their minds. I did not tell the students what I saw in my mind first. By choosing the text with this explicit purpose,

I made sure it contained enough images so that I did not have to think aloud *for* my students.

In the writing lesson, I intentionally used authors from the books the class had already read, so that we could now focus on them as writers. The texts evolved into "mentor texts"—texts that teach us. By constructing the lesson in this way, I gave students an opportunity to learn directly from these texts. They compared different endings to figure out how real writers end stories. Again, I did not have to tell them how to end stories; I provided them an opportunity to construct their own strategies for how to conclude stories.

Student Try-Outs

Before we send students off to try something on their own, it is often helpful for them to try on a concept as a group. This typically happens as a part of or just after our direct teaching. When I am teaching a lesson on making inferences, for example, I often have students try out the strategy in pairs. One of the ways I like to do this is with an excerpt from Chris Van Allsburg's book *The Sweetest Fig*. After we have read and discussed the story, I put up a transparency of part of the text. We talk about what we know about Monsieur Bibot. Students typically say he is a nasty man. I then have students read the excerpt in pairs and have them look for the clues that told them Monsieur Bibot is a nasty man, even though the author never explicitly says so. In this way, students get a chance to try out the strategy together before they go off and read independently.

A student try-out during our writing lessons takes on a similar form. In Debbie Fujikawa's third grade, for example, she examined how authors use sensory details in their writing to help us get a better feel for what their characters are experiencing. During the try-out time, she invited students to try it themselves. She had students read the drafts of fiction stories they were writing. After they read their drafts, they marked a place in their own writing where they could add more details about how their character looked, sounded, or felt. Then, on a sticky note, they added details they wanted to insert. They stuck that note right where they would put it in their draft. As students were working on this together on the carpet, Debbie circulated to support those who were struggling. After the try-out, a few students shared a place where they thought they could add details to their writing. By doing this activity, Debbie got a quick sense of what her students understood and where they struggled. This also gave the students a plan for what to do when they left the carpet to write independently.

Try-outs are a good way to give students some guided practice. It is also a time when we can gather valuable information about where students might struggle, informing us on how we will need to support them when they go off to work on their own.

Reflection and Segue to Independent or Small-Group Work

After students have had a chance to work on what we have taught, we need to close this phase of the lesson. There are a few ways to do this. In her book *Whole-Class Teaching*, Janet Angelillo closes her mini-lessons with a "charge to the class" and some closing directions. I like the simplicity of this. We need to conclude our whole-class teaching time by making sure that students know what we have been working on and what they are supposed to do when they work independently. Angelillo makes the good suggestion that we write the "charge to the class" on a sentence strip as a reference point.

In my own lessons, I ask students to make a mental plan for independent work time. Before they go to their seats, I have students first think quietly about what they will do when they get to their desks. Specifically, I want them to consider the whole-class lesson, the skill or strategy they tried out, or the needs of their particular piece of writing. Then I say, "Turn to your partner to discuss your plans for independent writing time." After we have a few share-outs, students quietly move to their seats to get started.

Whatever technique we decide to use as a segue, the most important thing is to close this part of the lesson and transition to independent work time smoothly.

Independent Work Time

For our students to become thoughtful, avid, and proficient readers and writers, they must have time to read and write on their own. All of the reading and writing lessons in the world will not help students who do not actually read and write. There are huge payoffs for doing independent work. According to researchers Anne Cunningham and Keith Stanovich, "We should provide all children, regardless of their achievement levels, with as many reading experiences as possible. Indeed this becomes doubly imperative for precisely those children whose verbal abilities are most in need of bolstering, for it is the very act of reading that can build those capacities" (1998, pp. 7–8). Doing a great deal of reading is essential for students to grow as thinkers and learners. And it is the one thing we can't teach—it is something they must do.

> For our students to become thoughtful, avid, and proficient readers and writers, they must have time to read and write on their own.

As writers, our students need time to write. How can we expect them to develop and express their thoughts clearly if they don't have an extended time to write? In *The Art of Teaching Writing*, Lucy Calkins notes, "If students are going to become deeply invested in their writing, and if they are going to live toward a piece of writing and let their ideas grow and gather momentum, if they are going to draft and revise, sharing their texts with one another as they write, they need the luxury of time" (1994, p. 186). There is no way students can become proficient writers without the time for this essential act. Being a writer means that you have time to write.

Time for Individual Students

Independent work time is the one time during the day when we get the opportunity to pay attention to students as individual learners. We don't usually get many chances to sit quietly with one child and work on things that are important only to him. When the class is working independently, however, we have an opportunity for one-on-one time with our students. This time also provides a natural way to differentiate instruction for the variety of learners in our classrooms. Because each student is working in a book or on a piece of writing at their developmental level, we are tailoring the curriculum to meet each one's specific needs. Finally, independent work time is the place where students build the stamina they need to read and write for sustained periods of time. This stamina is critical for student success on high-stakes achievement tests as well as in the content areas as students move to middle and high school.

Characteristics of Independent Work Time

- ❁ Students work independently.
- ❁ The teacher establishes predictable structures for handling common interruptions (arranging bathroom breaks, getting paper, managing books, etc.).
- ❁ The teacher is actively conferring with readers and writers.
- ❁ The room is organized to maximize student independence.

Lesson Reflection

At the conclusion of every lesson, it is imperative that we set aside a few moments for students to reflect on what happened during the lesson. This allows us to close the lesson in a way that reinforces big ideas while planting seeds for tomorrow's instruction. I always divide the lesson debriefing into two parts:

- Academic debriefing
- Social debriefing

Academic Debriefing

During my academic debriefing with the class, I quickly review what we did during the lesson and have students share what they learned. I may, for instance, have students share a place where they tried out a revision strategy in their writing. After a reading lesson, I might have them discuss places where they inferred specific things about a character in their book. The goal is not to rehash the entire lesson but to invite students to share samples of the thinking they did during the lesson and establish a sense of closure. It also enables us to discuss and mark places where students struggled so we can address them in the next day's lesson. This encourages accountability in students' independent work, provides us a place to see where students are struggling, and allows students to hear what other students are thinking. This interaction also enables us to plant the seeds of tomorrow's lesson.

Social Debriefing

We cannot depend on students to work with one another in respectful and productive ways if we do not establish an ongoing process for discussing how that work went. In a social debriefing, students first reflect and then talk about how they collaborated. If students were working in pairs, for instance, we would discuss their partner work. Debriefing our conversations allows us to raise the level of discourse in our classrooms. Debriefing our behavior allows us to work on our classroom community. By taking a few minutes after each lesson to talk about it, we send important signals to our students. We show them that we value relationships, we value communication, and we value our work. Operating in this way fosters a caring place where learning can thrive.

BENEFITS OF A PREDICTABLE STRUCTURE

Using a predictable lesson structure has a powerful effect on our teaching. In my early teaching years, I initially struggled because my students had no idea what was going to happen from one day to the next. My lessons unfolded differently from day to day, depending on my planning. There was little structure or predictability in what I was doing. Now we know that having a predictable lesson structure is essential to all of our students' success—and especially to our English language learners.

English Language Learners

Think of yourself as a newcomer to a country. Now consider what it would be like to go to school where you don't understand anyone. Think about what it would be like if, each day you showed up at school, things were structured a bit differently from the day before.

- How comfortable would you be?
- How would you know what was expected of you?
- How would you know what materials you need and when you need them?

One of the ways we can help decrease anxiety and increase participation by all students is by making our lessons follow a predictable structure. If every day we have students come into the classroom the same way, slip their backpacks on hooks, and take a seat on the carpet, students will get the hang of how to begin their day in our classroom. If during writing time we have students come to the writing corner at 9 a.m. with their writer's notebook and a pencil, it won't take long before all of the students are there with pencil in hand ready to write. In their book *Teaching English Language Learners*, Katharine Davies Samway and Dorothy Taylor support the idea that English language learners benefit from a predictable lesson structure in which teachers do the following:

- ✤ Keep to a scheduled time for activities so that children know what to expect
- ✤ Design specific locations for certain activities, which adds to the ELL child's sense of security about what to do in each location
- ✤ Use consistent language that helps students transition more easily from one location to the next (p. 49)

Using predictable structures helps ELL students become a part of our classroom. It gives them a chance to grow and learn just like the rest of the students in our rooms.

SUMMARY

When I was having trouble writing this manuscript a few months ago, I decided to talk with my colleague Stanley. He is the grant writer for our organization. His real work, however, is as a playwright. Stanley has written over 15 plays and has seen them performed all over the country. I was sure he could help. "Pete," he said. "You are so busy. I can't possibly imagine how you can write."

"How do *you* do it?" I asked.

"Well, you know, I work here only three days a week. I drive up to the cabin in Sonoma on Wednesday evenings and write until Sunday. I have structured my whole life so I can write."

When Stanley left my office, I remember wondering how I could convince my wife that I needed a cabin in Sonoma to finish this book. I then thought about his words a bit more. I realized he was right. Maybe a Sonoma cabin was out of reach, but I did have to find a regular, predictable time to write. The book was not going to write itself. I realized that if I got to my office every morning around 4:30 a.m., I could have four quiet hours each morning to write. And write I did.

If we don't create predictable times and space to do the important things in our life, we simply won't do them. As teachers, we know this is true. With so many things crammed into our day, we simply won't get to the things we value if we don't structure them into the fabric of our teaching.

Try this . . .

Lessons that come out of our teacher's manuals rarely contain the structures outlined in this chapter. They contain many useful ideas and resources but are often organized in ways that are not clear and predictable. As you try to bring more structure to your teaching, it will be helpful to try to incorporate the structures outlined here into your lessons. In order to do this, take out a lesson from one of the teacher manuals you have. First, read the entire lesson. After you finish reading, take a pencil or sticky note and try to identify the following parts of a lesson:

• Preparation for work

• Whole-class teaching time

• Independent work time

• Lesson reflection

If you don't find a place in your written lesson for one of these parts, mark where you can insert it.

In this chapter, I shared a predictable structure you can use to plan your literacy lessons. Having this structure to ground our teaching allows us to focus ourselves more on how students are making sense of the information we are providing. It enables us to center our lessons on the needs of our students. The structure gives us a place to put all of the wonderful content we want to share with our students. Having a predictable structure is critical as we move on to rethinking lesson planning, which we cover in the next chapter.

Chapter 3

Lesson Planning: A Fresh Look

Lesson planning may not be the most glamorous thing we do as teachers, but when we do it thoughtfully, it becomes one of the most important. For many years as a teacher, I never thought much about my own planning—I just did it. It was a rote activity for me. The teacher's manuals I used contained most of the directions. I took time every Sunday to jot down in my plan book the goals for each of the week's lessons. I recorded textbook page numbers and story titles. I then looked through my teacher's manuals to see what might need extra preparation. I noted things like setting up experiments, organizing manipulatives, and arranging art supplies. That was the extent of my lesson planning. By early Sunday evening I was ready for my week.

There is nothing really wrong with this form of planning. My teacher's manuals contained a great deal of content to cover. And by following them, I was complying with my state's standards—certainly a critical lesson element. But looking back on it, I realize my planning was incomplete. I was merely "scheduling" my hours and days.

When I review my old lesson plans, I realize that the most important component of teaching—my students—was missing from my preparation. When I was planning lessons on those Sunday afternoons, I was only doing a fraction of what the job required.

Recently, during my years as a staff developer, I have given lots of thought and consideration to what lesson planning could entail and how to create a planning process that brings out powerful teaching. As teachers, we do so much more than simply cover content; our jobs necessitate that students access this content. Consequently, we cannot limit our planning process to mere scheduling, writing down lists of what to cover, and collecting and preparing materials for a given lesson. In powerful planning, we need to consider the nuanced moves that make the biggest difference in our teaching. We want to make the best use of our programs and materials and turn our lessons into meaningful experiences for our students. To do this, we must have a more dynamic and thoughtful lesson-planning process that goes beyond identifying content and that helps us envision what might happen when our students face that content.

One of the consequences of the legislated education reforms of the past decade is that teachers have been forced to follow lessons in comprehensive reading programs verbatim. In this way, the programs end up doing a great deal of the thinking for the teacher. One refrain I hear often in my travels from district to district is "Why should I plan the lesson when it is all written here?" As explained earlier, rotely following programs is problematic for the simple reason that these preprogrammed lessons do not take into consideration the students we teach. At the same time, the reality is that many of us need to use the programs our districts have adopted. Given these district and/or state constraints, what we must do then is implement a more powerful planning process to transform those programs into meaningful teaching.

This chapter shares the thinking that my colleagues and I have done to reconsider the lesson-planning process. Though it may be unrealistic to plan every lesson of every day with the level of detail outlined here, the goal is to try it with a few key lessons each week. In rethinking lesson planning, we have tried to improve the way we bring our students into the process of crafting lessons. This process has transformed our interactions with students, and subsequently their interactions with one another.

FIVE STEPS TO POWERFUL LESSON PLANNING

My most meaningful work as a staff developer has centered on planning sessions with individuals or groups of teachers. As part of this process, I use a modified version of the "lesson study model" (Lewis, 2002; Richardson, 2004) of staff development. Lesson study comes to us from Japan, where "lesson studies" are the core of the Japanese teacher's professional development (Lewis, 1995). It is a powerful model because it helps teachers continuously self-reflect and revise their teaching. The process starts with a team of teachers who meet to collectively plan a lesson. The teachers then observe the lesson being taught by one of the team members. Finally, they reflect on the student thinking and behavior they observed and revise the lesson accordingly. As I work through a similar planning process with colleagues, we increase our ability to be responsive to the needs of our students while we immerse them in the required content of our grade levels.

When I debrief these staff development sessions with the teachers, they inevitably comment on how powerful the lesson planning process was. Teachers in one group noted, "We never planned a lesson in quite this way before. It changed the way we see our teaching. We were able to trace our students' thinking and behavior back to the decisions we made as a group when we planned." This process of planning, reviewing, and revising our instruction is the basis for the following five-step planning process.

Important Planning Note

The five steps in the planning process that I outline in this book begin after you review the lesson in your teacher's manuals. (If you are a workshop teacher, you can use this process after you review the mini-lesson you have already written or have taken or adapted from a professional resource.) Before beginning the planning process, it is critical to fully read your lesson to be clear about the goals for what you're about to teach. If you have crafted your own lesson, review it to make sure you understand the content. Once you have reviewed the lesson, gather all the materials you need for the lesson. (You might, for instance, need a particular trade book or set of books.) By reviewing a completed lesson in advance, you can then use these five steps to revise your teaching to focus better on your students' thinking, and thus become more intentional about the specific teaching moves you envision making in the course of your teaching moments.

Step One: Establish the Lesson's Purpose

A lesson's purpose is centered on specific goals. These goals serve as a beacon to keep us on the right path as we travel through the course of a lesson. It keeps us from losing focus due to the myriad potential diversions we face during our actual teaching moments. To serve as this guiding light, our goals need to be clear, concise, and achievable. Otherwise, our goals could have the opposite effect and take us away from where we want to go with our students. In *On Solid Ground: Strategies for Teaching Reading K–3*, Sharon Taberski writes the following on setting lesson goals:

> I try to be realistic about the goals I set and hold myself strictly accountable for helping children achieve them. It's counterproductive to have too many goals and later abandon them because I'm overwhelmed by the inevitable demands of the classroom. So I limit the number of goals I set, and work seriously and purposefully on each one. (p. 9)

This is wise advice. Ms. Taberski understands how critical our goals are for our teaching. She also understands that the goals we select for our lessons need to take into consideration the standards required for our grade level as well as our students' needs. The relationship between our lesson goals and student needs is a dynamic one. Somewhat like a weighted balance, they continually tug at one another. We cannot plan good lessons without considering them both.

Academic and Social Goals

When planning lessons, we craft two types of goals—academic and social. Having dual goals ensures that both of the things we value— how students are working together and what they are learning—are given equal attention during our teaching.

Most teacher's manuals have lists of academic goals for each lesson. Whether you use Lucy Calkins's *Units of Study* or McGraw Hill's *Open Court* reading series, all programs have explicit lesson goals that can get you started. When I select the academic goals, I try to rewrite them in the form of a question, a concept I borrowed from esteemed authors Yvonne and David Freeman. In their book *ESL/ EFL Teaching*, they share a powerful process for planning called the "Questioning Lesson Plan." When our goals are stated in the form of open-ended questions, we then know they are rich enough for a lesson or a unit-long inquiry. The box below offers examples of academic and social goals crafted in the question format.

Examples of Academic Goals Stated as Questions

- In what ways can we infer cause and effect?
- How do we visualize as we listen to a story?
- What are some ways we can explore how different authors begin personal narratives?
- How do we correctly punctuate dialogue?
- What are some questions/wonderings we have as we read? How do these questions/wonderings help us understand the text?
- What opinions/positions can we develop around this nonfiction text?

Examples of Social Goals Stated as Questions

- How can we agree and disagree respectfully in discussions?
- How might we share work equally?
- What tools can we use to help extend one another's thinking?
- How can we give and receive peer feedback respectfully?
- How can we listen to one another respectfully?
- How can we reach agreement?

One challenge that teachers often encounter in creating goals is that most programs list far too many goals or objectives for each lesson; therefore, it is important to consider only those goals that you feel confident you can achieve and that meet your instructional aims. This gets sticky when we consider all of the standards we need to cover in the course of a year, which is why many programs pack in so many goals and objectives for each lesson. However, while this allows the programs to comply *on paper* with the standards set by our states, the programs do not effectively address real-life teaching or the needs of the students we teach. As teachers, we know we are most effective when we shape our lessons around one or two targeted goals.

As we plan, we must also remember that simply covering a standard just because it appears in the next lesson does not mean students will understand it or are ready for it. Conversely, eliminating a standard is obviously not an option either. There are numerous expectations for teachers to cover standards in a timely and scheduled manner. We must also remember that our students take tests that are linked to those standards. As teachers, we need to strike a balance between what our states require and what our students are ready for at the moment we are teaching. My not-so-simple advice is to know the grade-level standards well and to remember that we have an entire school year with many opportunities to cover them.

> As we plan, we must also remember that simply covering a standard just because it appears in the next lesson does not mean students will understand it or are ready for it.

Debbie Lera, in her book *Writing Above Standard*, helps us think about this particular balance in her discussion of writing standards. She encourages us to "Consider the power of writing that relies upon a standards-based foundation while still addressing the need for active learning through student inquiry. In this approach, you can use the structure provided by your standards but move within that structure in a way that allows you to respond naturally and genuinely to your students" (pp. 19–20). We cannot get lost in the trees of our daily lessons because we are not seeing the forest of our entire school year. We can take the resources we have and establish goals for our lessons that are both in tune with our standards and that meet the needs of our students.

Another challenge teachers face when establishing goals is that most programs do not have explicit social goals. To craft these goals, we must reflect deeply on what social skills our own students currently need to work together successfully during a specific lesson. Just as students come to us with a variety of academic skills, they also come with a range of social skills. If we want students to push one another's thinking, they need to learn the social skills that will help them do this.

Helping students develop these skills takes time. It is often necessary to work on one specific social skill over the course of a few weeks. In Gail Fay's sixth-grade classroom, for instance, one of the social skills she worked on with her class was "How students can get 'unstuck' when their partner discussion fizzles." She spent a few days brainstorming with her class various strategies they could try to get "unstuck." Gail recorded these strategies on chart paper and encouraged her students to try them out each day. As the unit progressed, she continued to check in on which strategies were working for the students and which ones were not, and eventually they had a near-final list that worked for the class. In all, Gail's process took a few weeks before it made a significant impact on the class's partner talk. But by focusing on one specific social goal that the class would work on, the group reached a typically challenging social goal with great success.

Guiding Questions for Developing Lesson Goals

These are some questions that teachers have found helpful in paring down their lesson goals.

- Of the goals listed in your program materials, which one seems the most critical and appropriate for students in your class?
- What is the one thing, above all else, that you want to make sure you cover during your lesson?
- How does today's goal fit with the lessons that preceded it?
- How might we write these goals as questions?

Step Two: Create a Plan for Introducing the Lesson

A strong beginning to a lesson will help ensure that our students will stay with us as we move into the body of our lesson. An effective introduction will do two important things:

- Establish the academic focus for the lesson and prepare students for the content that will follow
- Prepare students to work together

Establish the Academic Context

When we plan our lessons, it is essential to establish a clear way for the students to connect the content of the lesson to what they have already been studying. We know that meaningful learning does not happen in a vacuum. Therefore, we need to ensure that today's lesson is clearly related to yesterday's and will connect to what will follow tomorrow. Janet Angelillo calls this part of the lesson the "orientation" or "link." She says that in this part of a lesson, "The teacher reorients students to learning by reminding them of previous lessons, referring to recent charts and discussions, and/or citing books they've read or studied" (2008, p. 47). We must execute our lessons in a way that helps students connect and activate the current content in their minds. This is also the portion of our teaching time when we clearly convey to students what the objective for the lesson is.

> **Teacher Might Say:**
> *This week we have been drafting our personal narratives. For the past couple of days, we have been looking at how Jerry Spinelli and Patricia Polacco begin their stories in ways that hook the reader. Yesterday, you all tried to learn from them by trying out three or four different leads. I wonder what those same authors can teach us about how to end our writing? Today we will look at how authors end their pieces.*

Build Background Knowledge and Vocabulary

After we consider how we will orient and begin our lessons with our class, another thing to consider is what background knowledge and vocabulary might pose challenges for students. For example, if I am reading aloud or using an excerpt from a trade book, I need to make sure all of my students will be able to access the text. Once I have identified the background and vocabulary I think my students will need, I then decide which specific ideas and words to teach. This task is not so easy; just because a word or a concept is challenging does not necessarily mean we should spend time teaching it. Though some words might be difficult for your students, they might not be critical to understanding the text. In other words, there are concepts that are challenging, yet they do not impact understanding of the lesson's objective. Therefore, we must make the difficult decision of whether or not to include them in our teaching.

Lesson Planning Example

Our class has been working on a memoir genre study. The goal of this lesson is for students to examine how professional writers use the setting in their own narratives. The students will then take this learning and see how they might describe settings in their own narratives. To do this, I decide to use the book *Bigmama's* by Donald Crews. I am using Mr. Crews's book because of his wonderful description of the summers he spent on his grandmother's farm. I want the students to pay particular attention to the ways in which he makes the farm (the setting of the story) come alive.

As I read this story during my planning session, I notice that there is a reference to segregation in one of the drawings at the very beginning of the story. (Crew's family has traveled in a segregated train car on their way to Bigmama's farm.) I recognize that this is a particularly difficult concept, and I know that it is a concept my students don't fully understand. What do I do? Do I spend time talking about segregation and help build background? I would love to dive into this topic but I wonder if this is the right moment to do it.

One way to help make a decision like this during your planning session is to review your lesson's purpose. In this example, my goal is to examine ways authors describe setting and use setting in their personal narratives. Because this is my goal, I realize that the students do not need to fully understand the concept of segregation to understand the story and to achieve the lesson's goals. Teaching about segregation in the middle of a writing lesson will take up too much lesson time, and it will most likely keep me from getting to the heart of the lesson. More important, the concept of segregation surely requires separate time to do it any justice. In the end, I decide I will not specifically teach the concept of segregation during this teaching moment. I do, however, plan to go back to this text when we revisit segregation as its own topic.

Decisions such as the one I describe are hard to make. But it is important to remember that we simply cannot do everything during our limited teaching moments. In fact, when we try to do it all, we run the risk of diluting our teaching with lots of content, doing none of it well, and failing to help our students reach our goals.

Tips for Providing and Activating Background Knowledge

- Decide what students need to know to access the lesson.
- Start by having students say what they know about a topic. This can be as simple as asking, "What do you know about . . . ?"
- Provide only the information that your students absolutely need to know. This should be done clearly, directly, and succinctly.
- Consider that if you must spend more than a few minutes introducing background knowledge, perhaps it needs its own separate lesson.

Tips for Introducing Vocabulary

• Only preteach those words around concepts that are critical to students' understanding of the topic. Most of the time, vocabulary can actually be addressed during the body of the lesson. English language learners, however, may benefit from prereading texts, using pictures, and discussing words before they encounter them with the rest of the class.

• Avoid "fishing" for answers. Instead, simply give students the meaning of a difficult word or concept. When I started out as a teacher I used to handle vocabulary like this: "Who knows what *photosynthesis* means?" I called on students around the room, "fishing" for the right answer. Later I realized that this takes lots of valuable time away from the actual lesson and causes confusion for students. Teach vocabulary quickly as you encounter it in the context of the lesson. You can do this efficiently and fluidly by giving students the definition of a word and continuing with the lesson. If your lesson contains the word *audition* and you suspect most of your students don't know what the word means, instead of asking, "Who knows what *audition* means?" you might say, *"Audition*—audition is when you try out for a part in a play." Then move along with your lesson.

• Create a "Vocabulary Parking Lot" chart for listing important words that you do not have time to address during the current lesson. The Vocabulary Parking Lot serves as a reminder when planning separate future lessons. This list can be as simple as a piece of chart paper hanging on the wall. When you get to a word you want to add, you simply write in on a sticky note and place it on the chart paper. At the end of the day, or when you are gathering vocabulary words to teach, you can look in the "parking lot" for a list to teach. Once you teach the word, you can pull it off the chart.

As you plan to build background knowledge and vocabulary for your lesson, ask yourself these questions.

- Given my lesson objectives, do my students need this knowledge to access the text?
- What background knowledge or vocabulary do my English language learners need that is different from what my other students need?
- How will I introduce this vocabulary?
- When will I teach this—during the lesson or before the lesson begins?

Prepare Students to Work Together

Students need opportunities to work and talk together. Students in classrooms that foster these working relationships often do better academically, and they develop important prosocial skills, including the ability to identify problems, develop strategies for dealing with them, and put in motion a plan for improvement (Kagan, 1997). Working well together is a skill essential to academic success (Duke & Pearson, 2002; Freeman & Freeman, 1998). If we want to ensure that students get meaningful opportunities to work together, then we need to create a space for collaboration in our lessons. Unfortunately, many lessons are doomed from the start because well-intentioned teachers have included cooperative work without adequately planning how to best prepare their students for it. This section of the planning process is therefore dedicated to setting students up to be successful.

Lesson Planning Example

Last October, I planned to teach a writing lesson in a fourth-fifth-grade combination class. As I planned this lesson, I toyed with the idea of having students work in groups of four to brainstorm topics for a nonfiction writing project. My first task whenever I plan for partner work is to make sure the task is authentic. If students do not see a real need to work with partners, they might view it as "busy work," and the activity will be unproductive. My second task is to identify the academic and social skills that the students will need to be successful working in these groups. A quick rule of thumb is that if the social task is complicated, you want to make the academic goal easier. If the social goal is easy for students, you can have more challenging academic goals. My third task is to break down the social task to see if my students have the skills to handle it. This lets me know if I need to preteach a subset of skills to make sure the students are successful. In the case of this combination class, I discovered that in breaking down the students into groups, they needed to be able to do the following:

- Quickly get into their groups of four
- Determine who will record their brainstormed work
- Share their work fairly
- Include all members of their group in the discussion
- Understand the goal of brainstorming topics
- Understand the scope of the nonfiction project

As I reflected on this list, I was surprised at how many skills were needed and realized that the students had not yet mastered all of them. Because it was October, we had not had much practice beyond partner work. I began to worry that working in groups of four at this time might turn into a mess and jeopardize the rest of the lesson. Consequently, I decided to have students work in pairs—not groups of four—because they had much more experience working with just one partner. And by doing this, I felt that I could keep the lesson focused on brainstorming topics for independent writing.

Planning Questions for Introducing or Reinforcing a Social Skill or Cooperative Structure

Teachers can use this process to decide how to introduce or reinforce a social skill or cooperative structure. Ask yourself: What do students need to know to be able to use the structure or social skill? Do students have experience with the skill or structure?

My students do not have experience with the skill or cooperative structure.

- How will I introduce and model how to do this particular skill or structure?

- How can we all practice it quickly?

- What will I look for as students try it out? (What will the skill or structure look like when it is going well?)

My students have experience with the skill or cooperative structure.

- How familiar are they with the skill?

- What has worked/gone well in past lessons?

- What challenges have surfaced that the class is currently working on?

Step Three: Make Decisions Regarding How You Will Facilitate the Lesson

This step of the process involves planning how to teach the body of the lesson. Because this is the place where the lesson's main content is covered, there are many decisions to make. Below are some of the things we need to consider when planning this section.

❀ Of all the content in the lesson, what will we spend the most time on?

- Which parts of the lesson will be done in a whole group, small group, or independently?
- Where might students struggle? What can we do if they struggle?
- How do we facilitate the conversation in the lesson?
- How will the class transition to different parts of the lesson?

Decide What Content to Cover

Most lessons that come from reading and writing programs contain too many things to cover. Sometimes it seems like everything plus the kitchen sink has been thrown in. Our job is to sort through the content to pick the essential elements we want to cover. I always try to remember that less is more here. By having less in my lesson, I can spend time digging into it. If I have too much to cover, we rush to get through it and cover lots of ground—but none of it deeply. Recall Hilda Taba's wise counsel, "Don't cover the curriculum, *uncover* it" (1962)!

Decide How to Teach the Lesson

My rule of thumb is that if the content we need to address is not open-ended in ways that enable students to discover the answers, then we should teach it directly to students. When I rely on direct instruction to teach punctuation, for instance, I explain it clearly and quickly. Then I might give students time to practice using conventional punctuation in their own writing. If, however, we are studying the ways in which writers use white space in poetry, I might ask students to examine different poems and then invite them to discuss what they notice. I will chime in to push their thinking and add discoveries they don't find. The difference between these two lessons is the nature of the content. The content determines the teaching strategy or structure I might use—direct instruction is appropriate for one lesson; inquiry works best for another.

Envision Where Students Might Struggle

All students need to wrestle with their learning; indeed, such mental gymnastics—at times, a real struggle—is an essential part of the learning process. This is true for our high-flying students and the ones who lag behind. This is an important lens through which to view our teaching. When I was a new teacher, I wanted to avoid struggle at all costs. In fact, I was often frustrated when my students did not "get" something. Now I see struggle as a precious opportunity to peek into my students' thinking process. Ellin Keene sums this up best when she

> All students need to wrestle with their learning; indeed, such mental gymnastics—at times, a real struggle—is an essential part of the learning process.

writes, "If we can learn to see adversity as opportunity in our lives and in our classrooms, perhaps we will come to view challenges, comprehension problems, and other obstacles as fascinating intellectual opportunities to face together" (2007, p. 63).

A critical piece of planning, therefore, is anticipating what students might say or do in the lesson. This allows us to identify places that may be easy for some students and difficult for others. If we identify certain parts as easy or simply not challenging enough, this is a signal that we might be able to move more quickly through that part. Additionally— remembering that struggling is a part of learning—we might also want to raise the level of difficulty so that it is not so easy for students to work through. On the other hand, if we think students might struggle because the content is much too hard, then we can craft an alternative plan. We might decide to reread the story, or slow down to spend more time in a specific area.

Plan to Facilitate Student Conversation During the Lesson

Facilitating student conversation in a way that encourages our students to do most of the talking and thinking in our lessons is one of the most difficult tasks we have. A good facilitator understands that student conversation is the time when students make public the thinking they are doing silently in their heads. When we facilitate well, we get students to push one another's thinking. We get a front-row seat that allows us to look into how students are wrestling with the content at hand.

The starting point for any well-facilitated conversation rests in the questions we ask. Asking questions that get students to think deeply is challenging. I like to take time during my planning to jot down a few open-ended questions. This prevents me from getting stuck in the middle of my lesson without solid questions to ask. Sometimes I must rewrite questions from the programs I use. Other times I need to come up with questions all on my own. Either way, it is important to do before the lesson starts.

> **Note to reader: See Chapter 4 for teaching techniques and strategies for becoming a better facilitator.**

Plan Transitions

Transitions can be like quicksand. They are places in our lessons where students can easily get stuck. If I start my lesson on the carpet, we need regular routines and procedures to assemble there in an orderly fashion. If, after a whole-group lesson, we are going to transition to independent reading or writing, we once again need smooth procedures to get us where we need to go. Planning our transitions is the key to smooth success.

Step Four: Decide How Students Will Share and Reflect on Their Work

In Step Four, as we near the end of the planning process, we will look closely at the conclusion of a lesson plan. In Step Two, we spent time thinking about how to *introduce* the academic and social content of a lesson. Here, in Step Four, we will think about how to *debrief* those same academic and social areas with our students. This part of the lesson should not take a great deal of time—certainly no more than ten minutes. Nevertheless, it is essential and serves as a powerful bookend to our lesson, giving it a sense of closure. At the same time, it plants the seed from which tomorrow's lesson can begin to grow.

Plan to Debrief the Academic—Who Will Share and for How Long?

If we want this section of the lesson to be quick yet meaningful, we need to give careful consideration to how and what we want our students to debrief and share. For instance, in a writing lesson, if every student reads his or her entire piece of writing, we will need far more than ten minutes. And we know that if a sharing and debriefing segment goes on too long, our students can easily lose interest and our lesson may disintegrate. Therefore, to keep the lesson debriefing focused and engaging, it's helpful to refer once again to your lesson's purpose.

If a lesson's goal is for students to make inferences about characters in their stories, then one choice is to invite just a small group to share— those students who actually marked their inferences in their own books. Alternatively, you might randomly choose a few students to share out. Or you might decide to ask students to share with their partners. This choice ensures that each of your students will get a chance to share with someone, yet it takes the same amount of time as having only a few share with the class. Whatever you decide, the key is to keep this segment of the lesson brief and focused on your lesson objectives.

Plan to Debrief the Social—Sharing How We Worked Together

How did it go with your partner today? This is often how I start this segment of my lesson debriefing with the class. If we expect students to practice a social skill or cooperative structure, it is essential that we plan for how we will follow up to see how it went. We also need to remind ourselves that we should not expect things to always go smoothly with our teaching. When students struggle, they are showing us what they don't yet know or don't know how to do. We want our students to voice what is not working so we can work together to figure out how to solve the problem.

To set the debrief up for success in a particular second-grade class, I leaned into one partnership that was struggling and said, "I see that you both are frustrated because you spent most of your talk time trying to figure out who should talk first. Please bring that up when we debrief so we can hear about some ways other pairs are making it work."

I intentionally did this to send the students two messages. The first is that it is okay to struggle, that others might be struggling too, and together we can figure this out. The second message was that they cannot waste their partner time. When they were bickering about who should go first, they were clearly not on task.

At other times in the school year, especially in September, I have asked the question *How did it go today?* The students might all say "Fine." We know that responses like "Fine" get us nowhere and are probably not accurately describing the actual turn of events. When this happens, I might say, "I noticed that in some partnerships, when one partner was talking, the other partner was looking away. When you look away from your partner who is talking to you, how do you think your partner feels?" After we discuss briefly, I would then ask, "How should we respond when our partners are talking to us?"

After the class discussed this, I then charted their ideas about what they could do when their partner was talking. I can then refer to the chart at the beginning of the lesson on the following day. Day one's debrief of the lesson's social element leads to day two's lesson introduction.

Step Five: One Last Review

Step Five is the last step of the planning process. It is a step that teachers rarely incorporate in their lesson planning, yet, in my work with teachers, it is the step that oftentimes has the biggest impact on instruction. In this last stage of the planning process, before we enter our classrooms, we dedicate time to reflect on our lesson plan. By going back and systematically analyzing our plans, we might identify gaps, conflicts, or pacing and timing issues that we did not catch when we initially planned how we might teach this lesson.

Revise for Time

In every workshop I teach, I always ask teachers to name the biggest challenges they face. Inevitably "lack of time" appears somewhere near the top of that list. We have so much to do and our days are so short, we hardly have time to eat half a sandwich or even sit down to breathe for five minutes. It is an issue we constantly face.

One way I have found to address time constraints is to have teachers focus their lesson review around time. When I sit with a teacher in this stage of the planning process, I ask her to go through each part of the lesson and jot down how long she thinks each section will take to teach. Typically, we are shocked when we look down and do the math. Though we originally allocated 45 minutes for the entire lesson, after we review the timing, it appears that the teaching will need at least 65 or 70 minutes. This important review then forces us to make some decisions about how to pace the lesson:

- Where do we want to spend most of the lesson time?

- What do we have to cut so that we are spending the most time where we need it?

Before I got in the habit of reviewing and revising my lessons around time, I had far too many teaching moments. I would look up at the clock and realize that the science teacher would be in my room in two minutes, or that it was time for recess—and I was not near the end of my lesson. This typically happened because I spent too much time in places that were not the main focus of the lesson. I was trying to teach everything I could. I learned the hard way that I had to keep certain parts of my lesson short, or cut other things altogether, so I could spend most of my time in the places that counted most.

When we review our plans, we need to be judicious about where we decide to spend our valuable time. And if we keep the lesson's purpose at the heart of our planning, we are more inclined to focus our teaching and make the necessary cuts to keep our lessons well paced.

Revise for Areas Where Our Students Might Struggle

In Step Three of the lesson-planning process, you already envisioned places where your students might struggle. This helped you plan the lesson to meet the needs of your students. Now, as you review your lesson plan, you will want to focus your review on all of the places where students might encounter problems. Students might, for example, have a difficult time with a new social skill. They might also struggle with a difficult text. In reviewing all of these places, you can now decide if you are spending the right amount of time on each section of your lesson. This allows you, once again, to adjust your time accordingly.

When I taught fourth grade in New York, my class explored different types of nonfiction writing. One of the projects we took on was to write about the evolving role immigration plays in the state's history. We decided to do this through the lens of our own families. Some of my students' families had been in New York for generations and some had only arrived that school year. The students spent the first few weeks of the project collecting their own family stories as well as notes on immigration in general. One key lesson in that project was designed for students to organize their notes and begin their drafts.

When I started reviewing my lesson, I realized that many of my students did not collect enough family information or notes on immigration to begin their drafts. They needed more time to finish collecting information. I envisioned that they would struggle immensely if I went forward with this lesson. So, in reviewing my plan, I postponed my lesson on drafting and allowed one more week for students to collect stories and data. This decision made all the difference in their eventual success with the writing lesson.

I learned how important it is to review my lesson plans and to think through places where students might struggle. The following are three things I have learned to do when I review a lesson, to help me reflect on and better understand my students' needs.

- **Look over students' work at the end of the day to assess their instructional needs.** By doing this, we get a glimpse of what they know and where they are struggling with what we have already taught.

- **Review notes from conferences with students.** Our conferences are filled with information that is critical to understanding what our students do well and where they need more help.

- **Consider how students struggled, and why.** Sometimes I find it helpful to make a simple chart of the things students struggle with from a specific lesson. I keep a clipboard near me with a sheet of paper divided into squares. Each square has a student's name on it. If I notice a student struggling with something during a lesson, I quickly jot it down in the box. This allows me to see trends across the day.

Revise What We Will Say (Reducing the Number of Words We Use in Our Teaching)

One of the things that I admire most about my wife Nina's teaching is how she talks to her students. There is poetry in the way she engages them. One of the key reasons for this is not *what* she says but *how little*. It is through the economy of her language that she keeps her lessons flowing, her students engaged, and her instruction focused. I am consistently impressed with her style because I realize what many observers might not—that it is quite hard to teach this way. As writers know, addressing a key point within one paragraph is much more challenging than doing it in many pages. It usually takes revision to reduce your words from a whole page down to a paragraph. Teaching with this conciseness is equally challenging.

During planning sessions with teachers, I ask them to rehearse what they plan to say during key junctures in their lesson. I might say, *Pretend I am your student. Tell me exactly what you will say to encourage me to talk with my partner.* During these rehearsals, the teacher may become flustered and realize she is not quite sure how she will instruct her students. During an actual teaching moment, uncertainty often leads to a lot of unnecessary teacher talk. Rehearsing helps us clarify our teaching language and teaching moves.

Being clear and concise during our teaching, however, is difficult. To do it consistently, teachers need to be conscious of the language they use, be ready with the most important points they want to get across, and know their students. When we review our lessons and rehearse what we will say before we teach our students, we become conscious of and confident in our instruction; in other words, we become *intentional*.

Try this . . .

Use the Lesson Planning Process Guide located in the Appendix (pp. 109–110) to plan a reading or writing lesson. After you plan the lesson, consider the following:

- How much time do I have to teach this lesson?

- As I review my teaching plan, is it too complicated?

- Does the plan meet the needs of *all* of my students?

SUMMARY

Rethinking lesson planning and using the five-step process in this chapter allows us to take the necessary time to fully envision our lessons and to maximize the opportunities through which student thinking can thrive. It has helped me focus not only on the content I have to teach but also on the way I am going to deliver that content. When we devote time to planning, reviewing, and revising *before we teach*, we strengthen our instruction, and our students grow.

As We Teach

The first two parts of this book covered the teaching moves we make before the lesson starts. I made the case that the more intentional we are in our planning, the better we can focus ourselves on students' thinking and behavior. Part III of this book is dedicated to the decisions we make in the course of our teaching. Chapter 4 shares important facilitation techniques that help us push and support student thinking. Chapter 5 makes the case that we cannot do any of this work if we do not first attend to the classroom community.

Chapter 4

Lesson Facilitation: Deepening Students' Thinking

When I was a young boy learning the essentials of baseball, my dad taught me to play shortstop. The most important thing I learned was that in order to be successful, I had to start with the right stance—both mentally and physically. Before the pitcher threw the ball to the batter, I had to think about what I would do if a ball were hit to me. *Would I throw it to first or second base? How many outs were there? Were there runners on base?* Then I had to get my body ready to field the ball. I was taught that as soon as the pitcher started winding up, I was to move my glove toward the ground between my legs, and shift my weight to the balls of my feet—a position that allowed me to easily reach any ball that was hit near me. During practices, when I did not have the right stance, I often made mistakes. I either threw the ball to the wrong base or I missed the ball completely.

As I reflect on my own teaching, I see parallels between this baseball stance and the stance I need to deliver effective lessons. When I facilitate lessons, I need a stance—both physically and mentally—that allows me to be ready for the myriad challenges my students present during any given teaching moment. If I'm not ready, I may miss valuable opportunities to push student thinking.

The two previous chapters in this book focused on steps we take to prepare for instruction. Now I will take a closer look at unpacking the critical moves we make in the actual moments of our teaching.

Even if we are equipped with strong lesson plans, if they are poorly executed, we will not have a positive impact on our students' learning. In fact, the quality of our lesson facilitation is just as important as the plan itself. Step Three of the lesson-planning process (Chapter 3) briefly discussed facilitation. In that step, a teacher specifies the content of the lesson and determines how he or she will cover it. Most important, in Step Three the teacher identifies one or two essential questions that will guide the bulk of the lesson's discussion. The challenge lies in keeping the lesson focused on these essential questions in the midst of the actual teaching moment.

> Even if we are equipped with strong lesson plans, if they are poorly executed, we will not have a positive impact on our students' learning.

In this chapter, I will address how to facilitate lessons effectively by developing a teaching stance that helps to fully engage students and, at the same time, helps teachers fully engage, too. We want to facilitate in a way that encourages a lot of diverse participation and holds students responsible for their own thinking and behavior. We also want to encourage multiple interpretations so that we can dig deeply into our topic.

Here are some of the key aspects of effective lesson facilitation:

- Embracing situations where students do not know the "right" answers

- Listening to our students and exploring strategies for being a better listener

- Presenting ways to craft and deliver open-ended questions that encourage student thinking

- Exploring the powerful effect our words have on student thinking and behavior

CRAFTING A NEW STANCE: VALUING THE MOMENTS WHEN STUDENTS DON'T KNOW THE ANSWERS

The first step toward being a good facilitator is being mentally prepared to explore our students' thinking. Let's remember that it is the thinking our students do that is most important; therefore, we need to listen closely to the way our students connect concepts, explore ideas, and use their imagination, so that we have a window into what they are really learning. This can feel uncomfortable at times. When students start talking about the big ideas in our curriculum, there is no script for how it will go.

I can remember the first time one of my middle school classes discussed the book *From the Notebooks of Melanin Sun* by Jacqueline Woodson. This story, about a boy's relationship with his mother and the secret he discovers that has the potential to unravel their family, provoked many strong and varied opinions from my students. The issues of race and sexuality that students confronted presented many challenges for me as a facilitator. The challenges I faced included these:

How do I handle racist or homophobic comments from students?

How do I help students disagree respectfully?

How do I make sure we hear a diversity of opinions?

How do we build consensus?

When is it okay to move on?

How do I keep from swaying student opinions with my comments?

Some of my colleagues wondered why I would take on this challenge at all. They suggested I pick "safer" books—ones with less ambiguous truths and less tension. I knew, however, that the comprehension challenges the class encountered as we discussed the book were necessary for developing the critical-thinking skills they needed. An additional benefit my class received through discussions like this was that it strengthened our classroom community.

As we facilitate lessons, we need to have this mental stance so we can best help our students through challenging moments as they try to make sense of the content we have presented. Although their answers ultimately matter, these answers do not compare to the actual thinking behind their conclusions. As esteemed Harvard professor Eleanor Duckworth points out, "The virtues involved in not knowing are the ones that really count in the long run. What you do about what you don't know is, in the final analysis, what determines what you will ultimately know" (1987, p. 68).

This is perhaps the biggest lesson I have learned in my teaching. It has been my experience that when we are confronted with challenges in life, it is not how much we know that helps us address our challenges, it is our creativity, mixed with lots of trial and error (in other words, our ability to think and learn), that helps us solve our most difficult problems. In fact, most of the problems we face in our work and in our personal lives have no clear "right answer." There are typically many paths we can take to solve them. Our challenge is to find the solution that works best, given the conditions we are working under. Though we know this to be true, unfortunately, in many of our classrooms the "right answer" is often more valued than the process students used to come up with those answers.

Most classroom interaction is limited to recitation (Tharp & Gallimore, 1991). Recitation is when the teacher provides content (from lecture or texts) and then asks students questions. The students then show their mastery of the content (or the lack thereof). Curriculum taught in this way is focused on repeating information the teacher delivers, rather than on engaging students in meaningful talk around difficult concepts or ideas. This problem has been compounded in the past decade because of the No Child Left Behind policies. Because of the pressures of high-stakes testing, teachers have been forced to reduce their curriculum to the content that will be tested (Alvarez & Corn, 2008). This form of reductionist teaching will not prepare our students for the real challenges that await them in the working world.

To be successful in our world, students need to be able to process lots of complex information quickly and effectively. In an article in the *Harvard Business Review* (November 2007), David Snowden and Mary Boone discuss how business leaders must understand complexity as an essential task in leading their organizations. The 21st-century workplace requires more than knowledge of facts. If we are to prepare our students to succeed, they will need to use their imagination to see patterns and to link concepts. Therefore, as teachers, we then need to ask ourselves questions such as these:

Do I teach in a way that fosters investigation and inquiry?

Do my lessons inspire students' wonder and imagination?

Do I build the skills of persistence and stamina that rigorous thinking requires?

To foster this type of teaching, we must position ourselves in a manner that best encourages and supports the sense-making our students are doing. We need to craft a stance that allows us to move instruction beyond the simple call and response, and toward fully engaged conversations.

Why Knowing Answers Is Overrated

At this point, I should make it clear that I don't believe "correct" answers are absolutely unimportant. They certainly do matter. However, "right answers" too often become the major emphasis and priority in our schools. We know that real learning rests within real thinking. But, if we teach with a stance that only values reciting "right answers," then we will surely miss opportunities for investigating students' thinking. And in the end, we will end up listening only to what our students *say*, as opposed to what they are *thinking*. As Dr. Duckworth points out, "Knowing the right answer requires no decisions, carries no risks, and makes no demands. It is thoughtless. It is automatic" (1987, p. 64).

To illustrate this point with some teachers I once worked with, I passed out two students' final drafts of a writing assignment. I asked the teachers to review each work and tell me what they thought about the students as writers. When I asked for comments, it was clear that the teachers felt that one of the students' pieces stood out over the other one. They thought it was more structured and had more descriptive language than the other piece.

I then passed out all of the writing that went into creating the final drafts. This included notebook entries, multiple drafts, and the teacher's conference notes. Now the teachers had a chance to see all of the decisions that went into the final pieces. It turned out that the student with the stronger piece did not write much each day of the genre study, and she did not try many of the strategies the teacher introduced. She clearly wrote the draft a few days before the class published. But—because she is a strong student—she ended up with a coherent piece. Unfortunately there was not much evidence that she grew as a writer during the six-week genre study.

On the other hand, the teachers could quickly see that the student whose work they initially thought was the weaker writing of the two had worked harder and had done more thinking than the other student. This student grew by leaps and bounds. Some of the earlier drafts were actually much stronger than the final version. But because she took a daring chance to incorporate a writing structure the teacher recently introduced, her final version turned out not to be as coherent as she might have liked. Nevertheless, for this particular unit of study, she shone as the stronger student. This surprised the teachers and changed their opinions about the student's writing.

I used this activity to illustrate that if we look only at the final version—or the "right answer"—we run the risk of not seeing or valuing all student learning. It is the thinking and learning, along with the chances students take, that also need to be valued.

TEACHING ON THE EDGE OF YOUR SEAT

When facilitating lessons, one way to position yourself—perhaps figuratively and literally—is on the edge of your seat. In this chapter's opening, I talked about how it is helpful to stand on the balls of your feet when you play shortstop. This allows you to move in any direction from moment to moment. In teaching, our position as we listen and facilitate student thinking also dictates how we will be able to move with that thinking from moment to moment.

As you facilitate, here are some things you can do to stay "on the edge of your seat."

* Look directly at the student who is talking.

* Minimize outside distractions.

* Sit forward in your seat.

* Listen closely to your students.

* Explore and discuss the ways students come to their conclusions.

DEVELOPING LISTENING SKILLS

When my wife and I first moved in together, I discovered (perhaps I did not "discover" this—it may have been pointed out to me . . .) that I was not a very good listener. I had to learn that listening was different from hearing words. It did not mean nodding my head as I watched the Detroit Lions lose yet another football game. Listening meant tuning out football games, the newspaper, my Blackberry, and focusing intently on what my wife was saying. Anything less sent the message that the conversation was not important to me. I learned that people who listen do not multitask. The relationship we have with our students is no different. When our students are talking, we must listen. We cannot write a note to the office, quiet other children, or take attendance when our students are talking. We need to be present.

Perhaps we have never considered listening to be a critical teaching skill. We spend a lot of time asking students to listen to one another and are often frustrated when they do not. But it is equally crucial for a teacher to practice the skill of listening in order for a lesson to be successful. It is impossible to be good facilitators if we do not listen to what our students are saying. In her book *The Power of Our Words*, Paula Denton provides a unique perspective on the power that listening has on our instruction. She gives us six reasons why we need to listen.

1. Listening lets us know the child.

2. When we listen, children learn about themselves.

3. Listening builds a sense of community.

4. Listening makes our questioning more effective.

5. When we listen, students take their learning more seriously.

6. Our listening helps students become better communicators.

Listen First and Ask Questions Later

One of the most important components of being a good listener is not having a preconceived notion of what our students are going to say or "should" say. We should try to withhold judgment until after fully exploring students' thinking. In practice however, this is actually quite challenging. For example, sometimes we are so happy when a typically silent student musters the courage to respond that, after she shares her thoughts, we rush to add to what she says as a way to validate and support her. But we do this at the expense of missing out on probing her thinking around how she came up with her idea. Here is another way to approach it: Thank the student for sharing, and then, with great interest, ask her to share the thinking behind her idea. This not only validates the student for speaking up, but also invites her to "crack open her thinking." In this way, we demonstrate for the entire class the power of expanded intellectual exploration. Another example is the student who blurts out an answer before he actually thinks about a response. At first, the answer appears off topic and can color our impression of that particular student's thinking; indeed, we may turn our attention elsewhere and bypass an opportunity to discuss his thinking. These situations happen quite frequently in classrooms. Here is an example from a classroom I visited recently.

I was working with a team of first-grade teachers at a school in Washington. Together we planned a lesson on the comprehension strategy of visualizing. We decided to use the poem "Sliding Board" by Kay Winters (2001) as the primary teaching tool for the lesson. The poem uses figurative language to describe children playing on a slide. After we planned the lesson, one of the first-grade teachers bravely volunteered to teach the lesson for the group. The next day, we all crowded into her room to take notes on what the students did during the lesson.

As the teacher read the poem, she asked the students to use the words in the poem to give them a picture of what the author is writing about. She read the poem twice. After the second reading, she asked the students to turn to their partner to talk about the pictures they had in their minds. The students then quickly paired and talked. I was seated on the carpet next to two girls and listened in as they discussed the poem. One of the girls said, "I pictured that big curvy slide at the water park."

"Why did you picture that?" the other girl asked.

"Well, the poem said 'long thin ribbon ride' so I thought of that long one that whips you around."

"Yeah!" said the other girl. "I love that one."

After a short time the teacher called the class back together and asked, "What did you and your partner talk about?"

Many pairs talked about the first part of the poem "Swish wish down the slide." They talked about picturing in their minds children traveling down the slide. Some of the students visualized hair flowing in the breeze as children went down. In the middle of the conversation one of the girls I had observed raised her hand to share: "I pictured a curvy slide."

"Oh," said the teacher. "You must have used your background knowledge to get that picture. We have one of those curvy slides on the playground. So, you see, class, sometimes your background knowledge can help you get a picture of what you hear and read." The student just nodded. The teacher then called on another student to share.

When we debriefed the lesson, I read back the transcript of the partner conversation I observed, along with the transcript of what the teacher said. I asked the group what this made them think about. The teacher who taught the lesson said that because she was so happy that a normally quiet student participated, she jumped at the opportunity to validate the girl's thinking. After further reflection, she suggested wisely that she could have asked the girl, "What in the poem made you picture a curvy slide?" This same teacher pointed out that if she had probed the girl's thinking, she would have found out that it was a specific line in the poem that triggered the girl's visualization, not the slide on the playground at her school.

I do not know how many times I have done exactly what this teacher did. Instead of probing our students' thinking, we often assume we know what our students mean. As teachers, we are accustomed to thinking aloud in our comprehension instruction, and when we see the opportunity to connect thinking for students—we do it. Sometimes we do this at the expense of students doing the connecting and thinking for themselves.

This was the key lesson we all learned from this experience. We discussed the fact that sometimes during our lessons we are not listening for how the students visualized—we look only for the visualizations themselves. The group left this lesson study thinking about how to change our stance in lessons that would allow us to listen better and to probe our students' thinking.

Tools for Listening to Students

Actively listening to students is much harder than it sounds. Below are some ways I have found to focus more effectively on what our students are saying.

- **Take a few quiet moments to collect your thoughts before the lesson begins.** Right before I gather my students together, I typically take a brief moment to visualize what I want to happen. I think about the purpose of the lesson and remind myself to keep my students' thinking at the forefront of my mind. Through the busy, rushed, and interrupted days, it's important to take time to calm and focus ourselves before a lesson to help us listen better.

- **Take notes.** When I am facilitating a lesson, I always have a legal pad on my lap. I try to jot down things my students say that I want to remember. Sometimes in the middle of my teaching, I might pause to look over my notes. This allows me to bring my teaching back to important points that were brought up, and to keep the conversation focused.

- **Ask open-ended follow-up questions.** This allows me to make sure that I understand exactly what students are trying to get across. Through their explanations, I can get a closer look at what is really going on in their minds.

Remember your posture. We remind our students about how they should sit and behave when they are listening to another student. We, too, can follow these reminders. If we sit forward in our chair, poised to listen, we are more apt to be actively engaged. This helps us not only to look interested but also to stay fully engaged in what our students are saying.

CRAFTING OPEN VERSUS CLOSED QUESTIONS

As teachers, perhaps our greatest instructional tool is the open-ended question. Open-ended questions force students to dig below surface answers into deeper thinking. Open-ended questions do the following:

- Require more than one- or two-word answers
- Allow for multiple interpretations
- Encourage interaction
- Stimulate student talk
- Push student thinking

Observe the Kinds of Questions You Ask

The best way to improve the quality of your questions is by becoming completely conscious of them. To do this, you might try one of the following ideas.

- Jot down the questions you ask your students. This helps you stay focused on the questions as you ask them.
- Tape-record a lesson. You can then play it back later and focus on the way you asked questions. It also allows you to analyze your students' responses to the different types of questions.

❋ Ask a coach or trusted colleague to observe your teaching. Doing this gives you the opportunity to get another impression of the way you facilitate and question students.

Examples of Open-Ended Questions

• Why might the author have done it that way?

• What are some ways we might share our supplies?

• How can we make our visitors feel welcome?

• What did you notice about how the author described the farm?

• What are some of the things we know about tornadoes?

• What questions do you have?

Use the Power of Open-Ended Questions

In classrooms where students are accustomed to answering closed questions, they initially look for what they think the teacher wants to hear. Students are very conscious that certain answers are right and others are wrong, and they want to be right. This is why many of the conversations I observe in classrooms are reduced to surface-level talk and are extremely short. Students quickly try to lock into what they think the teacher wants to hear. As soon as someone gets the answer, the lesson moves on.

In classrooms where students are regularly asked open-ended questions, the students are more apt and able to explore ideas with one another. They begin to understand that we value their risk taking and their creativity. They know that it is okay if they try out an idea that turns out to be wrong. They are comfortable knowing that a classmate might help with another idea. In these

> In classrooms where students are regularly asked open-ended questions, the students are more apt and able to explore ideas with one another.

classrooms, students know that a lesson revolves around investigation, not just answers.

This point was driven home for me last spring when I observed Lindee Witt's fifth-grade class in Clark County, Nevada. They had just been discussing the causes and effects of earthquakes, using the nonfiction book *Earthquakes!* by Seymour Simon. At the end of this reading lesson, students were debriefing how they worked together. During the debrief, a girl said, "I noticed that when we disagree with each other, we are not disagreeing with the person. No one took it personally when someone had another opinion. A lot of us were not sure we understood why earthquakes happen. There was a lot of agreeing and disagreeing. When we agreed and disagreed, we ended up getting to what might be the real cause of earthquakes."

Lindee's students were clearly accustomed to responding to open-ended questions. She spent the first seven months of school asking deep questions, probing their thinking, and having students reflect on their learning and behavior every day. Because they had lots of practice doing this, they were able to try out different theories and ways of thinking as they moved successfully through their lesson together.

FACILITATION TECHNIQUES

When I work on improving the professional development I provide to teachers, I often turn to one of my mentors, Shaila Regan. Her observations about my teaching almost always focus on the way I facilitate conversations. Whether I was working with students or a group of teachers, she would sit in the back with her notepad and record every question I asked. She would also try to record the responses to each question. Later, we would debrief my work. A recurring theme in her feedback was that I had to do a better job of pushing people's thinking. She suggested that the conversations I was facilitating could be much deeper than they actually were. It was Shaila who taught me that a few core facilitation techniques could transform the work I did with adults as well as students. Now I use the following techniques to facilitate any conversation:

- Probe student thinking with open-ended questions

- Use wait time wisely

- Connect student thinking

- Use cooperative structures

- Use nonjudgmental responses

Probing Student Thinking

Probing student thinking allows you to see how your students came up with their ideas. When we probe student thinking, we uncover exactly how a student made sense of something. Math teachers know the value of this. Most math textbooks give students the answers because understanding math goes beyond a simple answer. Math teachers know that it is how we get to an answer that makes all the difference. Did the student guess? Did he or she memorize the fact? Or was the answer achieved through real problem solving? In literacy, probing student thinking is similar to asking students to "show their work" on a math problem. In addition, sometimes students' ideas that we initially judge as off target may actually be relevant once we become privy to their thinking. Consider the following example.

I once modeled a lesson in a kindergarten classroom in Vallejo, California. I read to the class the book *Where Once There Was a Wood* by Denise Fleming. The book follows a predictable pattern that starts "Where once there was a wood a meadow and a creek/ where once the red fox rested and closed his eyes to sleep." The book concludes "Where once there was a wood a meadow and a creek/ sit houses side by side twenty houses deep."

As I closed the book, I asked the class what they were thinking about the story. Some wondered why a town was built where the animals lived. Others wondered where the animals went once the houses were built. Toward the end of the discussion, one student in the back of the room raised his hand. "My dad is a firefighter," he said.

"Uh . . . okay," I responded. Then I paused. His comment seemed a bit off topic from what we were talking about. As I paused, I had two thoughts. On the one hand, this student could be having what I call a "5-year-old moment"—he just wants to talk and contribute something but really has no connection to the story. On the other hand, I wondered if perhaps there was something behind the comment. I decided to probe his thinking. I asked, "What in the book made you think of your dad's work as a firefighter?"

"Well," he said, "you read that the houses took away the animals' homes. But my dad fights forest fires and sometimes fires take the animals' homes away."

I was quite surprised by the complexity of his response. In actuality, this student had been synthesizing pieces of the story. He first inferred the point of the book—that through building houses we are destroying animal homes. He then brought his background knowledge from his father's firefighting to the text and interpreted that another way forests are destroyed is through fires. I would have missed this revelation had I thanked him for sharing and moved on. Instead, by probing his thinking, I learned that this kindergartner had been exploring complex ideas and inferences, and these thoughts could help the others in the class.

Examples of Open-Ended Probes Into Student Thinking

- What in the text made you think that?
- Say more about that.
- How is what you are saying different from (Mark's) comments?
- Why do you think that?

Using Wait Time Wisely

Wait time is an essential facilitation technique. Wait time gives students an opportunity to mull over a question and possible responses before they reply. Instead of jumping in after each comment students make, we can wait and give time for students to respond to one another. This helps our classroom through the students' ideas rather than through us. In his book *Choice Words*, Peter Johnston calls this wait time "thinking time." He writes, "Sometimes 'wait time,' the attentive silence after a child's comment, might better be called 'thinking time.' On the face of it, remaining silent seems trivial, but research shows that extending thinking times is positively correlated to more student talk, more sustained talk, and more 'higher order' thinking" (p. 56).

In many classrooms, however, wait time does not exist. According to Myra and David Sadker, "On average, teachers wait only nine-tenths of a second for a student to answer a question. If a student can't answer within that time, teachers call on another student or answer the question themselves" (1995, p. 57). The authors go on to say that "Waiting longer for a student to answer is one of the most powerful and positive things a teacher can do" (p. 57). This is especially important given the diverse nature of our learners. If we want to hear from many different voices and give all students a chance, we must use wait time after asking a question. Struggling students, quieter or more passive students, and English language learners all need time to process questions before they respond.

Using wait time also puts the responsibility for thinking back on our students. By pausing after we ask a question, we send the message that we expect a response. In my experience, when teachers become uncomfortable with the silence that follows a question, they usually bail their students out by giving the answer or by simplifying the question. Wait time helps set high expectations and helps establish a thoughtful tone in the classroom.

Connecting Student Thinking

Students often say things in the midst of our lessons that might be closely related to a comment made by another student. Though we teach students how to connect their ideas to others' by using discussion prompts like "I agree with . . . because . . . ," or "In addition to what . . . said, I think that . . . ," sometimes our students do not see the connections. This is where we, as facilitators, might want to step in and deepen a discussion by helping connect related ideas.

I recently observed my colleague Christine teach a fifth-grade class in which the class was discussing a picture book set in Nazi-occupied France. During the conversation, one student said, "I can't believe the police came to Helen's door to look for people. They must have been scared." Another student later said, "I think it was wrong for them to take Lydia back to her family. She could have been safe if she didn't go home."

As Christine listened to the students talk, she realized that the students were making some strong, thoughtful comments but they were not using these comments to dig deeper in the text. Sensing this, she said, "We heard Michael talk about how scared the family was when the police came to the door. We also heard Sarah say that it was wrong for Helen's family to take Lydia back to her family because she would have been safer where she was. What do you think they should have done? Why?"

This is an interesting example of how a teacher can connect two students' points to generate a deeper discussion. In this class, the students discussed the differences in the feelings of people hiding for their lives and those who were hiding them. Through the connection, they were able to dig into the issues around hiding during the Holocaust and the complex feelings the characters must have been experiencing. As an effective facilitator, Christine was able to connect two thoughts from different parts of a conversation and encourage a more productive discussion.

Using Cooperative Structures

Cooperative structures are a powerful tool for facilitating discussions. When I facilitate discussions, I typically use two structures—Turn to Your Partner and Think, Pair, Share.

⊛ **Turn to Your Partner.** Teachers first make certain that students know beforehand who their partner is. The teacher asks the class a question and instructs students to turn to their partner to discuss the question. For example, the teacher might ask the class, "Why might Charlotte feel sad? [Pause for a second.] Turn to your partner." After the pairs have had a chance to talk, the teacher signals them to return their attention to the whole group.

⊛ **Think, Pair, Share.** This structure is very similar to Turn to Your Partner. With Think, Pair, Share, after asking a question, the teacher offers a brief think time before instructing students to talk to their partners. This additional think time is helpful when students need to reflect on an idea or work through a complex issue. A teacher might say, "Think . . . What are you wondering about the story right now? [Pause for 10 seconds or so.] Turn to your partner and talk about what you are wondering."

As a facilitator, these two deceptively simple structures can help you in a variety of ways.

⊛ When you come to a point in a lesson when very few students respond to a question, you might use Turn to Your Partner to help stimulate thinking.

⊛ Conversely, when all of your students want to share in response to a question and you don't have enough time to hear from everyone, you might use Turn to Your Partner. This gives everyone a chance to share their ideas with someone, all in the same amount of time that it would take for two people to share with the whole group.

- Some students may be shy or quiet and not participate often in whole-group discussions. Cooperative structures such as Think, Pair, Share offer these students a safer option for sharing their ideas.

- Cooperative structures also help our English language learners. Having students work with partners is critical to language development and success in our classrooms (Freeman & Freeman, 1998; Samway & Taylor, 2007; Hill & Flynn, 2006). These cooperative structures offer students an opportunity to share, with little pressure from the whole class.

Using Nonjudgmental Responses

Everything we say in front of our students carries a great deal of weight. That is why I cannot overemphasize the importance of being nonjudgmental. Students are very adept at reading into our language. Whether we condemn or praise a student's comment, everyone in the class takes notice. In a discussion, for instance, if we say to one child, "That's a great point, Anna!" and then we turn right around and say to another child who makes a similar comment, "Okay, Marc," we send a clear but unintended message to the classroom that we value Anna's response more than Marc's. Ultimately, we may offend Marc and discourage any further responses from him and from others. We also run the risk of making Anna feel that she must always give the right answer in order to get praise from the teacher (Gootman, 2008).

It is important for teachers to be consistently nonjudgmental in their responses and comments to children. In my work at the Developmental Studies Center, we recommend that teachers use the following guidelines for responding to students' comments.

- Try to acknowledge student contributions without conveying judgment.

- Avoid comparing one student's responses with another's; instead, respond with a simple "Thank you" or an open-ended follow-up question such as "Who has another opinion?"

- Try to be consistent with your facial expressions, such as smiling at all students when they respond.

Responding in these ways prevents students from inferring what the teacher thinks is the "right answer." It also keeps the students focused on the ideas themselves, rather than on the teacher's judgment of the ideas.

Try this . . .

Getting better at facilitating lessons can make a huge difference in your classroom. Here are a few ways you can try to refine your practice.

- Have a colleague or literacy coach observe one of your lessons and have her record each question you ask the students. Have her mark how many students talk after each question. After the lesson, sit together and examine the kinds of questions you asked.

- As you facilitate lessons, have a pad of paper nearby and mark how many boys and how many girls talk in a lesson. At the end of the day reflect on what this might mean.

- As you begin to use cooperative structures, circulate around the room to listen in on partnerships. Record what you notice about their talk and behavior. After a few days of recording reflections, sit and reflect on their implications for future lessons.

SUMMARY

The magical moments of meaningful learning in our classrooms come from the intentional moves we make in the planning and facilitation of our lessons. Although many teachers make it appear easy to create these magical moments, it is actually quite difficult. Good teachers work extremely hard to bring their lessons to life. They take a very specific stance as they teach their lessons, one which allows them to respond effectively to students from moment to moment. Their stance provides a framework for facilitating student thinking that helps bring students to their greatest learning potential and creates a shining learning environment.

Key recommendations in this chapter for planning and facilitating effective lessons include the following.

- ❋ Embrace a teaching stance that focuses on students' thinking first, and resist the temptation to look for the "right" answer.
- ❋ Emphasize the importance of listening to your students. Listening is a teaching skill that needs to be cultivated and practiced, by you as well as your students.
- ❋ Examine the importance of open-ended questions.
- ❋ Use facilitation techniques that deepen student thinking and engagement:
  - Probe student thinking with open-ended questions.
  - Use wait time.
  - Connect student thinking.
  - Use cooperative structures.
  - Use nonjudgmental responses.
- ❋ Understand the powerful effects your words have on student thinking and behavior.

So far in this book, I have spent time on how we organize and teach our lessons. Now I want to shift our focus to the classroom community as a whole. The next chapter explores the importance that our classroom relationships have on the ultimate success of our teaching.

Chapter 5

Classroom Community: The Foundation of Successful Lessons

WHY WE BUILD COMMUNITY

A few years ago, I worked in Brooklyn with a fifth-grade class on a genre study in memoir. During one of my visits, the classroom teacher and I pulled up to Sean, who was bent quietly over his writing, and asked what he was working on. He looked up and paused, as if he wasn't sure he wanted to share his idea with us. "It looks important," I said. After waiting for a bit, he started to talk about his notebook entry. He had written about his small, white, very old cat. "We couldn't find him on Friday," he said. "On Sunday morning my mom found him in the basement. He was dead." Sean looked down, played with his pencil, and was quiet for a minute. Then he added, "We think he was sick. It's good that he's no longer feeling bad, but I miss him."

Sean was writing a tribute to his cat and had included a list of his cat's funny antics. I was impressed with Sean, impressed that he had decided to write about something so personal, and impressed that he had decided to tackle a writing technique his teacher had taught earlier in the week. I asked if he would share his piece with the class and he agreed.

Later in the morning, when the teacher gathered the class for a share, Sean read his entry. One of his lines mentioned that his cat was named "Bunny." As he read it, some boys in the back of the room snickered, amused that a boy would call his cat "Bunny." Sean heard the snickers, and I could see his shoulders and head fall. Clearly embarrassed, he paused during his reading. The teacher then said, "Let him finish." Sean responded, "Nah, it's stupid anyway." He put his notebook down, half-smiled, shook his head, and stopped reading. Sean never got to the part about how sad he was that his cat had died. He never got to the part about how his cat kept him company most days when he was alone while his mom was at work.

Later, when it was time to choose a notebook entry to work on for publication, he refused to pick the piece about his cat—even though he had by far the most entries on it. He also refused to share again with the class. His writing became shorter, choppier, and less important to him. It seemed as if he had stopped caring.

This story illustrates the power that the classroom community has on our students. All it took for Sean to stop taking risks with his writing was a few unchecked snickers from the back of the room. This was not a serious incident of bullying, nor the kind of teasing that often makes students refuse to return to school, nor does Sean come across as an overly sensitive person. In fact, later that day you could see Sean playing basketball with the same classmates who laughed at his cat's name. The snickers, however, were indicative of a greater problem with the classroom climate.

> All it took for Sean to stop taking risks with his writing was a few unchecked snickers from the back of the room.

The issue for me was not that a few boys were insensitive. After all, behaving insensitively is something fifth-grade boys do all the time, and do well. When they act this way, however, they are showing us what they don't know—that their words and actions can hurt others. And when they do hurt another classmate, they need to take responsibility for it. Unfortunately, this teacher did not have a structure for addressing hurtful behavior with the class. She just told them to stop. Telling our students to stop a hurtful behavior is not teaching them how or why to stop. The teacher missed a great opportunity for this class to reflect on how their words and actions affect one another.

Sean's experience could have been an opportunity to bring the class together, to help kids learn something about the impact of their behavior, to help students learn to empathize with one another. No one in the room, except for Sean, knew the real impact of the incident; it wasn't recognized or acknowledged, so all possible learning opportunities vanished.

Subtle acts like this happen in our classrooms more than we realize, and they can have a detrimental impact on the learning that's possible. To grow as a writer, Sean needed to be able to share his writing. He needed thoughtful feedback. Additionally, the class could have benefited from the smart work he was doing. A learning opportunity was lost, and Sean's willingness to reveal personal feelings as a writer was also lost.

A CONTEXT FOR TAKING RISKS

If we want students to grow as thinkers, readers, and writers, then they must be able to share ideas that are important to them. Important ideas, like the death of Sean's cat, are often personal. They are sometimes painful. It takes a great deal of courage for students to share an untested idea, read a book well below their classmates' level, or share what they are insecure about with their peers. They risk looking dumb, saying something perceived as silly, and being alone in their thinking. In order to learn, however, these are the very challenges students need to embrace. Risk taking is essential to growth.

In *Every Child Learning: Safe and Supportive Schools*, a policy guide published by the Learning First Alliance, they establish that building a supportive learning community is essential to students' success in school. The guide cites a number of studies that illuminate the connection between a safe, supportive environment and various positive outcomes for kids. One of my mentors, Eric Schaps, the founder of the Developmental Studies Center and a national leader on character education, has published multiple studies on the importance of building community in schools. Specifically, Eric's work has helped educators understand that when schools help students develop a "sense of community," the students reap many benefits. These benefits include, but are not limited to, liking school better, increasing their academic motivation, becoming better at resolving conflicts, and improving their academic achievement (Schaps, Battistich, & Solomon, 2004; Schaps, 2005).

TIME FOR COMMUNITY

With the beginning of each new school year, a new community forms in our classrooms. This community is built both explicitly, though intentional structures and activities, and implicitly, through our tone, language, and behavior. Our best teachers understand this and manage their classrooms so that attending to their community is an integral part of all instruction. In these classrooms, community building is not regarded as an add-on or extra activity. It is woven into the fabric of classroom life. Unfortunately, when I walk into many schools, I still do not see much attention to community building.

In Making Meaning, a reading program that I helped develop, the first unit at each grade level is dedicated to community building. When I work with teachers on this program, however, I find that this chapter is often skipped. When I ask why, teachers say, "We want to get to the important stuff—the comprehension strategy work." They tell me that this is what is tested so it is what they teach. These teachers don't realize the fundamental mistake they are making in their teaching. They don't realize that they will never reach the depth of learning needed for success without establishing a caring community.

Although these teachers like the idea of community building, they do not know how to add one more thing to their too-full plates. This becomes one of our greatest challenges. We must find ways to integrate community-building tools, techniques, and structures into our lessons, to ensure that community building is not an afterthought. When we take the time to integrate community-building structures into our teaching, we can have a positive impact on student growth and achievement (McTigue, Washburn, & Liew, 2009). We ensure that incidents like the one I related earlier about Sean are rare, and if they do occur, they become opportunities for students to grow together instead of barriers to learning.

Classroom community building needs to be an explicit goal within our instruction, alongside the academic focus of our lessons. We cannot have one without the other. Community sets the stage for powerful teaching. Therefore, we cannot plan lessons in hopes that student thinking will shine in an environment where our students do not care about one another.

TOOLS FOR BUILDING A CARING CLASSROOM COMMUNITY

In the summer, when my wife, Nina, begins planning for the upcoming school year, she sits on the floor of our office in her cut-off jean shorts and T-shirt. She lays out her curriculum and envisions where she wants to take the students that year. She knows the state standards, the dates when district benchmark assessments are given, and some of the big content areas she must cover that year. She also understands that for students to be able to do the rigorous thinking that the curriculum requires, they must be able to work together to push one another's thinking.

The first thing Nina does in her planning is sketch out her first six weeks of school to make sure the students have the social skills they need to be successful. She also wants to make sure that she installs specific structures that initially build community and later help to sustain growth over the course of a very long year. She knows that she will need structures that allow her to solve the difficult problems that lie ahead. She uses tools such as these:

- Team builders
- Class meetings
- Writer's notebooks
- Read-alouds

She also attends to the social climate of her classroom through the inherent structure of her lessons. This is a critical step to ensure that community building is not an afterthought. The rest of this chapter will focus on these tools and how they help us create the context for powerful teaching.

Team Builders

Team builders are low-risk activities that allow us to focus on getting to know one another better. Many teachers do these activities at the beginning of the school year, before requiring students to work together in an academic setting where complicated content demands attention.

In Lisa Billings's second-grade class in Louisville, Kentucky, students sometimes do team builders as a part of their morning meeting. Recently, when I visited her classroom, she said to the children, "Today is the first day of spring. Do you prefer winter or do you prefer spring?" The students then had to make a choice. The students who preferred spring went to one side of the rug, found a partner, and talked about what they thought was great about spring. Those who chose winter retreated to another part of the rug, formed partnerships, and talked about their love of snow. After a quick minute, Lisa asked another question: "Let's think about spring. Would you rather plant a garden or fly a kite?" The students repeated the earlier process with this second question. At the conclusion of this five-minute activity, Lisa asked the class how they thought they did. Students thought for a minute, and then one student said, "We all listened to the question and found a partner. It was pretty noisy, though." Another student chimed in, "I could barely hear my partner—it was too loud."

"How loud should it be?" Lisa probed.

"Well," the student thought, "we should use soft voices so all partners can hear each other."

"Okay," Lisa said, "let's try that when we work together later today. One thing I noticed was that many of us went to the same partners we always go to. How can we mix things up better?"

The class thought, and then a girl in the back of the room said, "Let's make a new rule. Each time we choose partners, we must find a new person."

"Okay," Lisa said, "we can try that tomorrow."

Lisa's actions took the team builder from an ordinary activity to a different level. She used the team builder as a vehicle for students to work on their social interactions. For Lisa, a team builder is more than a simple, non-academic activity. A team builder is teaching time. Lisa intentionally sets up activities where students will inevitably struggle socially. The struggle is not something to punish, but an opportunity to help the students learn appropriate ways to interact with one another. In the middle of the activity, she could have frozen the class and told them they were too loud. She also could have engineered the partnerships herself. But by avoiding these things, she gave the students an opportunity to take responsibility for their own behavior. By debriefing the activity, she raised the level of student thinking. She also sent a clear message that working together is important, and the classroom community is always trying to find better ways to do it. Additionally, she set the stage for work they would do with reading and writing partners later in the day.

Although Lisa included this activity as part of her morning meeting and did not have an academic focus, this kind of activity also has lots of possible connections to academic work. Other teachers might use this activity in an academic area.

Often, when I observe teachers engaging in team builders, it feels as if the teachers are simply going through the motions, to simply check off a box: "I did my beginning-of-the-year stuff. Now, I can move on to other things." Teachers who do a few team builders and then move on to the "real" work of school are missing the deeper meaning of team building. True team builders are not simply icebreakers; rather, they are opportunities for students to share who they are. They are part of a process to help students feel safe enough to talk about what is essential to them as learners. Team builders can serve as stepping stones to the deeper connections students will make over the course of the year. Below are three team builders that I use regularly with teachers.

* **Forced Choice.** A forced-choice activity, like the one that Lisa Billings used, gets students up and moving and interacting with one another. It can be a simple activity used to help students get to know one another. It can also be used to deepen student interaction around a content area. One might, for example, post four poems, one in each corner of the classroom, and have the students choose the poem they like best. When they form a group under a poem, they then discuss why they chose the poem. It is important to debrief the activity and ask students what they learned about their partner or members of their group.

* **Inside/Outside Circle.** In this activity, half of the students in the class form a circle facing out at the room. The other half of the class then forms a circle around the first group so they are each facing one person in the first group. The teacher asks a question, such as "What is the best book you have read this year? Why?" The students talk with the person across from them. After both students have had a chance to talk, the teacher instructs the students in either the inside or outside circle to take a few steps to the right. Now students will be facing a new partner. The teacher will then ask another question, such as "What is your favorite thing to do on the weekend?" The children discuss and continue the process for as long as the teacher wishes.

* **Partner Interviews.** The partner interview is an activity I like to do early in the year. It is essential that we give students many opportunities to work together in lots of different settings early in the school year. Whether it is to break down cliques, to get boys and girls to work together, or to help socially struggling

students work with others, partner interviews, and partnering, in general, help to build bridges between students. In the partner-interview activity "Talking Artifacts" (Developmental Studies Center 1997), students are asked to bring in special objects from home. The students then interview each other about these items. Finally, they share with the whole class what they learned about each other. This can also be done less formally, by having students ask simple questions of each other, such as "What is your favorite after-school snack?" Any question that helps students learn what they have in common with others—and helps showcase their special qualities—works well. The more opportunities students have to interact with one another, the closer they pull together as a classroom community. It also helps to establish a context of caring, which is necessary to help solve problems that will inevitably arise later in the school year. The information from these partner interviews can also be charted, graphed, and used in future lessons around collecting, monitoring, documenting, and analyzing data.

Resources for Team-Building Activities

Caring School Community by Developmental Studies Center (2004)

Blueprints for a Collaborative Classroom by Developmental Studies Center (1997)

Cooperative Learning by Spencer Kagan (1997)

The Morning Meeting Book by Roxann Kriete, Northeast Foundation for Children (2002)

The First Six Weeks of School by Paula Denton and Roxann Kriete, Northeast Foundation for Children (2000)

Tribes: A New Way of Learning and Being Together by Jeanne Gibbs, CenterSource Systems (1994)

Class Meetings

In a thoughtful teacher's hands, class meetings give students a voice in the decisions that affect them. The class meeting is a structure that helps students solve problems, make decisions, plan whole-class events, or check in on how things are going. We might have a class meeting to address better ways to share classroom materials, to discuss teasing on the playground, or to decide how best to welcome a new student into the classroom. The structure allows students to discuss issues in a context where the teacher can also help them learn the social skills they need to participate effectively. It is a powerful tool that is directly correlated with students' sense of community in their school (Schaps, Battistich, & Solomon, 2004).

Katie Von Thillo, a third-grade teacher in San Francisco, maintains that class meetings are one of the key reasons her class works so well together. Her class community is so strong that visitors from across the district come to observe her in action. She uses class meetings to solve some of the thorny issues that plague many classrooms. In her room, students discuss how to address arguing, fighting, or teasing in the schoolyard. She also uses the meetings to check in with the class at the end of the school day. It is a forum for her and the students to come together around issues the class faces.

Characteristics of Class Meetings

All class meetings share some common characteristics:

- The class sits in a circle.

- Clear ground rules are established.

- The teacher typically facilitates the meetings.

- Topics that matter to the whole class are addressed.

We never want to conduct a class meeting around a topic that only the teacher can solve; for instance, we would never turn over to a class meeting a problem with one student who was not sharing playground equipment fairly. Issues that involve only one or two students are not appropriate for a class meeting. Class meetings address whole-class issues. Similarly, we do not hold class meetings around issues that children cannot change. If, for example, the school rule is that students must walk quietly in the hall, we would not have a class meeting on whether or not we should walk quietly in the hall. Meetings must be about topics, events, and issues on which we are willing to let students voice their opinions.

Class meetings always have a predictable structure. The structure is learned early in the year and then repeated with any class meeting, no matter the topic at hand. The template that follows is one you might use or adapt to conduct your own class meetings.

Template for Class Meetings

Step 1: Review ground rules for the meeting (one person talks at a time, everyone looks at the speaker, no naming names, etc.).

Step 2: Gather the class in a circle.

- Make sure you establish a procedure for regularly and efficiently gathering the class in a circle.

- Make sure everyone can be seen.

Step 3: Introduce the topic.

- Clearly state the purpose of the class meeting.
  - You might say: *In today's meeting, we will check in on how things are going out in the yard during recess.*

Step 4: Discuss the topic/issue.

- Use cooperative structures to have students first talk in pairs.
  - You might say: *We talked last week about trying to include one another when we play outside. How are we doing? Turn to your partner and talk about that.*

- Discuss the issue as a group.

- You might say: *What is something you and your partner talked about?*

⊛ Probe students' thinking with open-ended questions.

- You might say: *Have you ever been excluded? How did that make you feel? What might you do if it happens to you or someone else?*

Step 5: Agree on next steps or solutions.

⊛ Reach decisions by consensus.

- You might say: *Is there anything on this list that you can't live with?*

Step 6: Reflect on the meeting.

⊛ Share what you notice about how students worked together.

⊛ Have students talk about how they worked together.

Step 7: Close the meeting.

Types of Class Meetings

⊛ **Planning/Decision Making.** Planning meetings allow a class to have a voice in some of the events that occur during the year. The class might meet to plan how to run the open house, for instance. If a teacher knows she will be absent one day and a substitute teacher will cover for her, she can use a class meeting for the students to plan how the day will go with a substitute.

⊛ **Problem Solving.** These meetings can prove the trickiest to facilitate, but are extremely important to the community. When the class is struggling with an issue such as teasing, bullying, or sharing, a class meeting helps students to examine and discuss possible solutions. It is not a tonic that makes problems go away overnight. It is a process for discussing, in a safe and respectful way, the issues the group may be facing.

⊛ **Check-In.** Check-in meetings are the most common meetings. Check-ins can take five minutes at the end of the day. Typically, these meetings have students share with a partner, and then a few students share with the whole group. These meetings are designed for students to talk about how things are going in the class. They might talk about their favorite part of this particular school day, one thing they learned, any issues the class is having, or their after-school plans. Finally, check-in meetings can be used to follow up on classroom issues. If, for example, students are working on better ways to share the playground equipment, then a teacher might check in at the end of the day to see if things are getting better. The class can use this time to add to and adjust the decisions they made, as they work toward an effective solution to the problem.

Writer's Notebooks

While a writer's notebook is an essential tool for the writing workshop, it also can serve as a powerful tool to bring the class closer together. As students generate ideas, reflect on experiences, and write about things they value in their lives, they learn more about one another as individuals. In my own classroom, when I had students read vignettes from their notebooks, they shared about catching their first fish, trying to sleep through hot summer nights, holding a baby brother for the first time, being scared of the dark, or winning a basketball game. Sometimes we laughed together, and sometimes we got quiet and sad together. Each entry uncovered a little bit about who my students were. So, while this is a key tool for the writing workshop, it also serves as a way to bring students together.

The sharing of notebook entries also provides us with opportunities to work on our community. To share the important things we write and to encourage students to take risks with their writing, we must have conversations about ways we can listen to one another respectfully. We talk about how we should sit, how we face each other, and how we might respond to one another. We ask students to visualize what it might feel like to share something special and have someone laugh or tease us. These discussions bring the class a little bit closer each time we share. It helps us empathize with one another and see past the surface issues to view each person as an important individual.

Read-Alouds

Of all the things we do in school, perhaps the easiest way to build community is through the read-aloud—inviting students to listen to and discuss books we read aloud. The simple act of students listening quietly together and then talking about their ideas brings a group together. When I read aloud Robert Munsch's *We Share Everything!* with first graders, the class rings with laughter. When I read aloud Francisco Jimenez's short memoir *The Circuit*, fifth graders share their reactions with tears in their eyes. In both instances, students become more interdependent, more empathetic. By talking about texts, they uncover bits and pieces of who they are, and they gradually feel more comfortable taking risks with their thinking.

Teachers I work with take care in selecting the titles they read, especially at the beginning of the year. Choosing texts that get students to giggle, make them sad, and fill them with wonder goes a long way in helping us bring students together. Selecting the right book actually does the hard work for us. It is a tool that helps us construct a learning situation for students that is rich and engaging and helps us hook the student to the task at hand. As Lester Laminack writes in *Unwrapping the Read Aloud*:

> To make the read aloud intentional, I believe that we must be as thoughtful in our planning as we are when selecting manipulatives for mathematics, or when establishing the flow of a classroom. We must select the books we will read with the same care we take in designing centers or in setting up a science lab. We must be as diligent in considering our reasons for reading aloud as we are in selecting the focus of a mini-lesson in reading and writing workshops.

In short, we must pay careful attention to our intentions for the read aloud. So why do we read aloud to our students? What are our expectations for the experience? What result or product do we hope for? How will our students be different for living through these experiences with us? (p. 18)

There are lots of resources for reading aloud to students. The quintessential text for reading aloud is Jim Trelease's classic *The Read-Aloud Handbook*. Anyone looking for great titles, read-aloud techniques, and rationales need look no further. Teachers looking for a great annotated list of titles they can use for different classroom purposes should turn to Lester Laminack and Reba Wadsworth's book *Learning Under the Influence of Language and Literature*.

CONCLUSION

In 2008, the *San Francisco Chronicle* ran a story about a first grader who was reportedly victimized at an Oakland elementary school. It was a disturbing account of bullying and violence at the school. According to the article, a first grader got into an altercation with a fifth grader and ended up in intensive care (Asimov, 2008). The same day, the *Oakland Tribune* shared some disturbing statistics from the school. "The school, with 344 students, had 312 suspensions last year, 97 of which were for violent incidents, according to the CDE report" (Bender, 2008). These numbers are staggering. How does this happen? I have spent the past few weeks haunted by the numbers, trying to understand the implications so many suspensions might have on a school.

Let's say for the sake of argument that for each act of violence that caused a suspension there had to be at least two students involved: the one suspended and another against whom the violent act was committed. That means that, at a minimum, 194 of the school's 344 students were involved in acts of violence that required suspension that year. If I add into the equation the number of kids who witnessed the events, who, one might argue, are also victims, the number jumps even higher. Finally, I thought about the number of nonviolent acts of bullying and teasing that may have occurred on the playground, in the hallways, and in the classrooms that go unreported, and my head started spinning. How are those students going to come into classrooms and do the thinking they need to be successful? What kind of after-effects do these events have on teaching and learning? Ask yourself what kind of impact this might have on a school. Does anyone think for a minute that students' thinking and in-school behavior are not affected by this climate? The Learning First Alliance reports, "Nationwide, 27 percent of teachers say that student misbehavior keeps them from teaching a fair amount to a great deal of the time" (p. A1, 2001).

Thoughtful, engaged learning occurs in classrooms and schools that support safety and community. To build community, we have to plan for it. It does not happen by accident. It is not easy to do. There is no magic formula for creating a safe and caring place. It begins the first day and requires attention every day until school is out. Relationships in our schools and classrooms are no different than other relationships in the world. If they are not consistently maintained, they can break down. None of the activities in this chapter, alone, will build the kind of classrooms we dream about. It is the combination of them that works together to create a caring place for children and adults. We can't expect students to take risks and dig deep in their souls to learn together if they do not care about one another.

Throughout this book, I have talked a great deal about the need to be intentional—about our academic objectives as well as our social ones. These intentional steps make the difference between lessons that shine with the brilliance of student thinking and ones that are void of imagination. It is our choice. We do make the difference.

Appendix

Asking yourself the questions at each step of the process will help you plan and stay on focus.

Lesson Planning Process Guide

Step 1: Establish the Lesson's Purpose

Academic focus

- What is the most important objective of this lesson?
- What is one thing I most want my students to take away from this lesson?
- How does this lesson fit with the lessons that precede it?

Social focus

- Given our working goals as a class and what this lesson presents, what is the social focus of the lesson?
- As a class, what social goals have we tackled?
- What new social focus should we work on?

Note: Decisions we make in steps 2 and 3 will impact these social goals. We may later choose to revisit and revise these goals.

Step 2: Create a Plan for Introducing the Lesson

- What background knowledge/vocabulary do my students need to access the lesson?
- What connects this lesson to previous lessons?
- How will I prepare students to work together?

Step 3: Make Decisions Regarding How You Will Facilitate the Lesson

- What parts of the lesson will be done as a whole group, small group, in pairs, or independently?
- Where would students benefit from working together?

- What cooperative structures will I use?
- What facilitation techniques might I use?
- What questions will I ask to stimulate student thinking and interaction? When will I ask them?
- Where might students struggle?

Step 4: Decide How Students Will Share and Reflect on Their Work

- What questions will I ask my students about what they learned?
- What questions will I ask my students about how they worked together?
- What will I do with this information?

Step 5: Review and Revise Your Teaching Plan

- How much time will each portion of this lesson take?
- Where do I want to spend most of my teaching time?
- Where in this lesson might my students struggle the most?
- What changes do I need to make in previous steps?

Teacher Reflections About the Lesson

- In my teaching, what went well today?
- What will I need to bring to tomorrow's lesson?

References

Alvarez, L., & Corn, J. (2008). Exchanging assessment for accountability: The implications of high-stakes reading assessments for English learners. *Language Arts, 85*(5), 354–365.

Angelillo, J. (2005). *Writing to the prompt: When students don't have a choice.* Portsmouth, NH: Heinemann.

Angelillo, J. (2008). *Whole-class teaching: Minilessons and more.* Portsmouth, NH: Heinemann.

Asimov, N. (2008, April 24). Oakland: When school bullies get out of hand. *San Francisco Chronicle,* p. A1.

Atwell, N. (1998). *In the middle: New understandings about writing, reading, and learning* (2nd ed.). Portsmouth, NH: Boynton/Cook.

Bender, K. (2008, April 24). Bullying incidents at Oakland grammar school spur special meeting. *Oakland Tribune.*

Calkins, L. M. (1994). *The art of teaching writing.* Portsmouth, NH: Heinemann.

Calkins, L. M. (2001). *The art of teaching reading.* New York: Longman.

Calkins, L. M. (2003). *Units of study for primary writing: A yearlong curriculum.* Portsmouth, NH: Heinemann.

Calkins, L. M., Montgomery, K., Falk, B., & Santman, D. (1998). *A Teacher's guide to standardized reading tests: Knowledge is power.* Portsmouth, NH: Heinemann.

Crews, D. (1991). *Bigmama's.* New York: Greenwillow.

Cunningham, A. E., & Stanovich, K. E. (1998). What reading does for the mind. *American Educator, 22*(1 & 2), 8–15.

Denton, P. (2007). *The power of our words: Teacher language that helps children learn.* Turners Falls, MA: Northeast Foundation for Children.

Denton, P., & Kriete, R. (2000). *The first six weeks of school* (Strategies for Teachers Series). Turners Falls, MA: Northeast Foundation for Children.

Developmental Studies Center. (1997). *Blueprints for a collaborative classroom.* Oakland, CA: Author.

Developmental Studies Center. (2004). *Caring school community.* Oakland, CA: Author.

Duckworth, E. R. (1987). *The having of wonderful ideas: And other essays on teaching and learning.* New York: Teachers College Press.

Duke, N. K., & Pearson, P. D. (2002). Effective practices for developing reading comprehension. In A. E. Farstrup & S. J. Samuels (Eds.), *What research has to say about reading instruction* (pp. 205–242). Newark, DE: International Reading Association.

Fleming, D. (1996). *Where once there was a wood.* New York: Henry Holt.

Fletcher, R. J. (1992). *What a writer needs.* Portsmouth, NH: Heinemann.

Fox, M. (1998). *Tough Boris.* New York: Voyager Books.

Freeman, Y. S., & Freeman, D. E. (1998). *ESL/EFL teaching: Principles for success.* Portsmouth, NH: Heinemann.

Gibbs, J. (1994). *Tribes: A new way of learning and being together.* Calabasas, CA: Center-Source Systems.

Gootman, M. E. (2008). *The caring teacher's guide to discipline* (3rd ed.). Thousand Oaks, CA: Corwin Press.

Hill, J. D., & Flynn, K. M. (2006). *Classroom instruction that works with English language learners.* Alexandria, VA: Association for Supervision & Curriculum Development.

Hoestlandt, J. (1995). *Star of fear, star of hope.* New York: Walker.

Jiménez, F. (1997). *The circuit: Stories from the life of a migrant child.* Albuquerque: University of New Mexico Press.

Johnston, P. H. (2004). *Choice words: How our language affects children's learning.* Portland, ME: Stenhouse.

Kagan, S. (1997). *Cooperative learning.* San Clemente, CA: Kagan Cooperative Learning.

Keene, E. O., & Zimmermann, S. (2007). *Mosaic of thought: The power of comprehension strategy instruction* (2nd ed.). Portsmouth, NH: Heinemann.

Kriete, R. (2002). *The morning meeting book* (Strategies for Teachers Series). Greenfield, MA: Northeast Foundation for Children.

Laminack, L. L. (2009). *Unwrapping the read aloud*. New York: Scholastic.

Laminack, L. L., & Wadsworth, R. M. (2006). *Learning under the influence of language and literature: Making the most of read-alouds across the day*. Portsmouth, NH: Heinemann.

Learning First Alliance. (2001). *Every child learning: Safe and supportive schools*. Washington: D.C.: Author.

Lera, D. (2009). *Writing above standard*. New York: Scholastic.

Lewis, C. C. (1995). *Educating hearts and minds: Reflections on Japanese preschool and elementary education*. New York, NY: Cambridge University Press.

Lewis, C. (2002). *Lesson study: A handbook of teacher-led instructional change*. Philadelphia, PA: Research for Better Schools.

Lowry, L. (2006). *The giver*. New York: Delacorte Books for Young Readers.

MacLachlan, P. (1993). *Journey*. New York: Yearling.

McTigue, E. M., Washburn, E. K., & Liew, J. (2009). Academic resilience and reading: Building successful readers. *The Reading Teacher, 62*(5), 422–432.

Miller, D. (2008). *Teaching with intention: Defining beliefs, aligning practice, taking action, K–5*. Portland, ME: Stenhouse.

Mochizuki, K. (1994). *Baseball saved us*. New York: Lee & Low.

Munsch, R. N. (2002). *We share everything!* New York: Cartwheel.

Obama, B. (2009, January 18). What I want for you—and every child in America. *Parade.*

Oppenheim, J. (1998). *Have you seen bugs?* New York: Scholastic.

Owocki, G., & Goodman, Y. (2002). *Kidwatching: Documenting children's literacy development*. Portsmouth, NH: Heinemann.

Ray, K. W., & Cleaveland, L. & (2004). *About the authors: Writing workshop with our youngest writers*. Portsmouth, NH: Heinemann.

Richardson, J. (2004, February/March). Lesson study: Teachers learn how to improve instruction. *Tools for Schools,* 2–8.

Sadker, M., & Sadker, D. (1995). *Failing at fairness: How our schools cheat girls*. New York: Scribner.

Samway, K. D., & Taylor, D. (2007). *Teaching English language learners: Strategies that work, grades K–5*. New York: Scholastic.

Schaps, E. (2005). *The role of supportive school environments in promoting academic success* (California Department of Education, Healthy Kids Program Office).

Schaps, E., Battistich, V., & Solomon, D. (2004). Community in school as key to student growth: Findings from the child development project. In J. E. Zins, R. P. Weissberg, M. C. Wang, & H. J. Walberg (Eds.), *Building academic success on social and emotional learning: What does the research say?* (pp. 189–205). New York: Teachers College Press.

Simon, S. (1995). *Earthquakes*. New York: HarperTrophy.

Snowden, D. J., & Boone, M. E. (2007). A leader's framework for decision making. *Harvard Business Review, 85*(11), 69–76.

Taba, H. (1962). *Curriculum development: Theory and practice*. New York: Harcourt, Brace & World.

Taberski, S. (2000). *On solid ground: Strategies for teaching reading K–3*. Portsmouth, NH: Heinemann.

Tharp, R. G., & Gallimore, R. (1991). *The instructional conversation: Teaching and learning in social activity*. National Center for Research and Cultural Diversity and Second Language Learning, Center for Applied Linguistics. (ERIC Document Reproduction Service, No. ED341254).

Trelease, J. (2006). *The read-aloud handbook* (6th ed.). New York: Penguin.

Van Allsburg, C. (1993). *The sweetest fig*. Boston: Houghton Mifflin.

Winters, K. (2001). *Did you see what I saw? Poems about school*. New York: Puffin.

Woodson, J. (1999). *From the notebooks of Melanin Sun*. New York: Tandem Library.